500 FACTS

Earth

www.pegasusforkids.com

© **B. Jain Publishers (P) Ltd.** All rights reserved. No part of this book may be reproduced, stored in a retrieval system or transmitted, in any form or by any means, mechanical, photocopying, recording or otherwise, without any prior written permission of the publisher.

Published by Kuldeep Jain for B. Jain Publishers (P) Ltd., D-157, Sector 63, Noida - 201307, U.P.
Registered office: 1921/10, Chuna Mandi, Paharganj, New Delhi-110055

Printed in India

 # CONTENTS

Preface 5

INTRODUCTION

Formation of Earth 6
Structure of Earth 13
Earth's Interior 23

EARTH AND ITS CONSTITUENTS

The Beginning 28
Fossils 37
Soil 47
Weather 52
Environment 58
Water Bodies 62

PHYSICAL GEOGRAPHY

Earth's Atmosphere 68
Moving Continents 73
Movement of Tectonic Plates 78
Mountains 84
Ice and Glaciers 89

Polar and Tundra Regions 94
Grasslands 99
Wetlands 104
Deserts 110
Forests 116

ROCKS

Rocks and Minerals 121
Formation of Rocks 133
Igneous Rocks 134
Metamorphic Rocks 144
Sedimentary Rocks 146

NATURAL DISASTERS

Hurricanes 151
Tornadoes 157
Tsunamis 160
Earthquakes 165
Droughts 171
Avalanches 174
Volcanoes 178
Floods 187
Extreme Temperatures 189
Wild Fire 191

PREFACE

There is no doubt that Earth is a unique planet. It is the only known planet to support various life forms. But Earth was not created in one day. Billions and billions of years of geographical evolution has gone into the creation of this great planet. Earth with its varying landscapes, life forms, water bodies, etc. has been a source of constant fascination and curious study for scientists and researchers. And the more you read and know about the Earth, the more there is to know. But why do we need to know about our planet? The study of Earth is important because Earth's history, evolution and changes in it are directly related to the past and present of existence of life. Information about Earth allows us to know how life came to exist on this planet and about the various phenomenon that affect and are constantly changing geographical aspects of Earth. 500 Facts on Earth attempts to get you curious about our vast planet with information presented in a fast-facts format. This book aims to improve your understanding of Earth. We not only aim to enhance your understanding of your planet, but also hope that these facts will help add value to your knowledge of many things around you.

Happy Reading, Kids!

INTRODUCTION

Formation of Earth

1 **Our solar system did not always exist as we know it today.** It may be hard to imagine now, but a few billion years ago, the solar system was nothing more than a giant rotating cloud of gas, rock and debris known as the Solar Nebula.

2 **Over time, the pieces of rock and debris smashed against each other, causing tremendous heat.** The heat caused these pieces to melt and become welded together. They grew in size until they were large enough to develop a magnetic force—or gravity.

FORMATION OF EARTH

3 Gravity attracted more materials and gas to gather into clumps that gradually got bigger, forming the planets in our solar system, including the Earth. This continued until the area around each planet was free of debris.

4 When two objects collide, their energy often turns into heat. This is what happened when the planets were formed. It is because of this reason that each time a meteor enters the Earth's atmosphere, the heat generated from its collision with air particles is so high that the meteor evaporates before it reaches the surface.

5 The Earth was formed by the coming together of various materials. Some of these materials were heavier than others. Gravity pulled the heavier materials to the centre to form the Earth's core. The rest of the materials formed the mantle, crust and atmosphere.

6 **The third planet from the Sun is Earth.** It is located at an ideal distance from the Sun. If it were any closer, the heat would burn everything on the Earth's surface. If it were any further away, its surface would be cold and frozen.

FORMATION OF EARTH

7 **Earth is the only planet in the solar system that is known to support life.** It has two things that allow life to exist: an atmosphere rich in oxygen and an abundance of water on its surface.

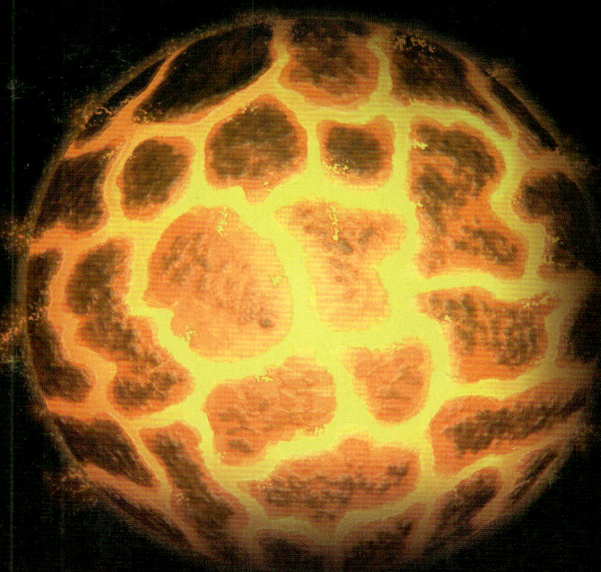

8 **Can you believe that Earth started off as a waterless mass of rock?** However, as the pressure deep within the Earth increased, it generated enough heat to melt the interior. This caused some chemicals to rise to the surface and form water.

INTRODUCTION

9 Meteorites are rocks from outer space that brush past the Earth's atmosphere and land on its surface. By studying pieces of meteorites, scientists concluded that the Earth was formed about 4.6 billion years ago. That makes the age of Earth about one-third of the age of the universe.

10 **The Earth is located at an average distance of about 150 million kilometres from the Sun.** Our planet appears bright and bluish when seen from the outer space. It is called the 'Blue Planet' because 70 per cent of its surface is covered with water.

FORMATION OF EARTH

11 **Scientists have discovered fossils in the depths of oceans—these are considered to be the first signs of life on the Earth.** These fossils are said to belong to some of the first multi-celled organisms that lived on the ocean floor, more than a billion years ago.

12 **Did you know that Earth is the densest planet in the solar system?** The density differs for each of its parts. Thus, the core is denser than the crust. But the average density of the planet is around 5.52 grams per cubic centimetre.

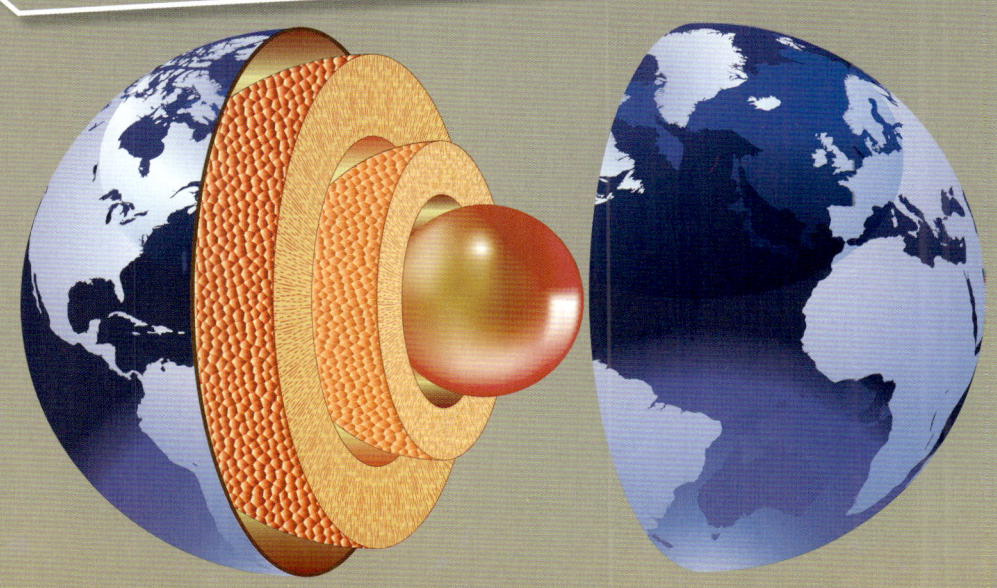

INTRODUCTION

CONTINENTAL DRIFT

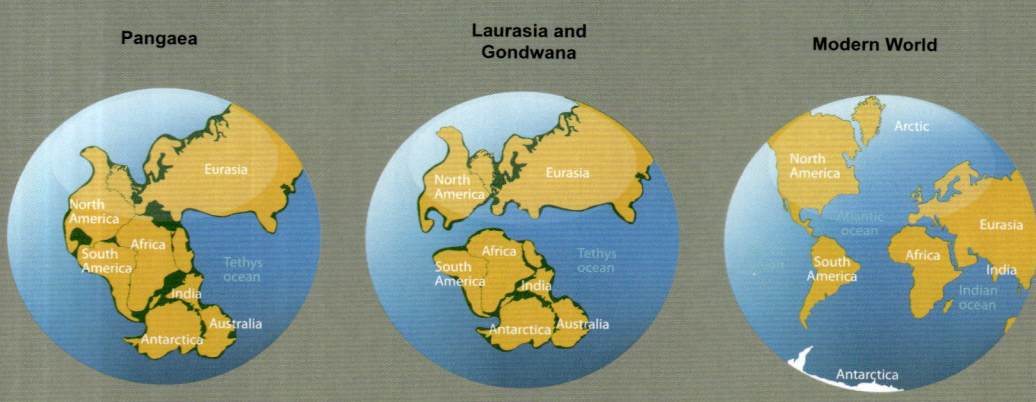

13 **When Earth first came into existence, the seven continents did not exist as they do today.** Instead, there was one large supercontinent called Pangaea that comprised all the Earth's land. About 180 million years ago, Pangaea broke into two landmasses—Laurasia and Gondwanaland.

14 **While Laurasia drifted to the northern hemisphere, Gondwanaland moved to the south.** Over time, both supercontinents broke into smaller chunks of land that floated across the globe to form different continents.

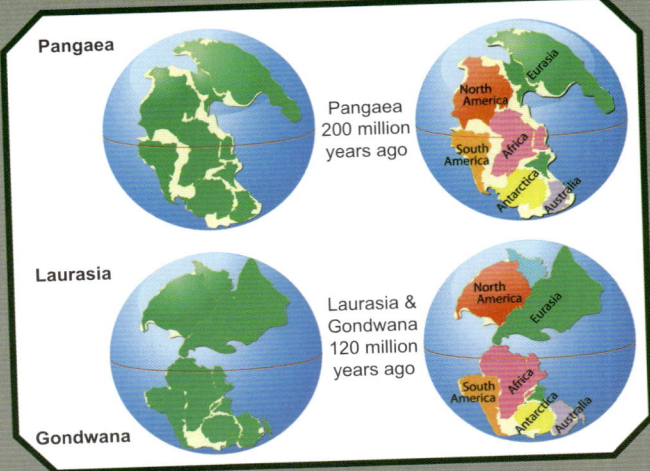

Structure of Earth

15 A long time ago, people believed the world was flat. In 1519, Ferdinand Magellan and his crew started a voyage around the Earth. Though Magellan died in 1521, his crew completed the voyage in 1522, thereby proving that the Earth was in fact, a sphere!

16 Ever wondered what makes the Earth round in shape? It is the invisible force of gravity that pulls the Earth into the shape of a sphere and keeps things in place on its surface. Without gravity everything around us would have floated away into space.

INTRODUCTION

17 **As the Earth rotates on its axis, it bulges around the middle, preventing it from being a perfect sphere.** Although that is a strange shape, we do have a special word to describe it. The correct shape of the Earth is called 'geoid'.

18 **Imagine a line running through the middle of the Earth and dividing it into two equal halves.** That imaginary line is called the 'Equator.' It lies at an equal distance between the North and South poles.

STRUCTURE OF EARTH

19 **The Earth is made up of many rocky layers.** The solid, outer layer is called the crust. Below the crust lies a layer of very hot, almost solid rock called the mantle. Beneath the mantle lies the core.

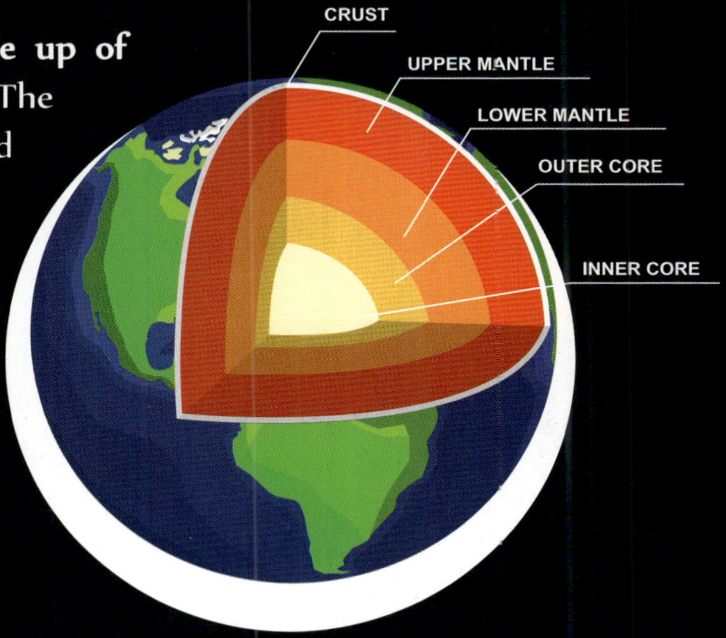

CRUST
UPPER MANTLE
LOWER MANTLE
OUTER CORE
INNER CORE

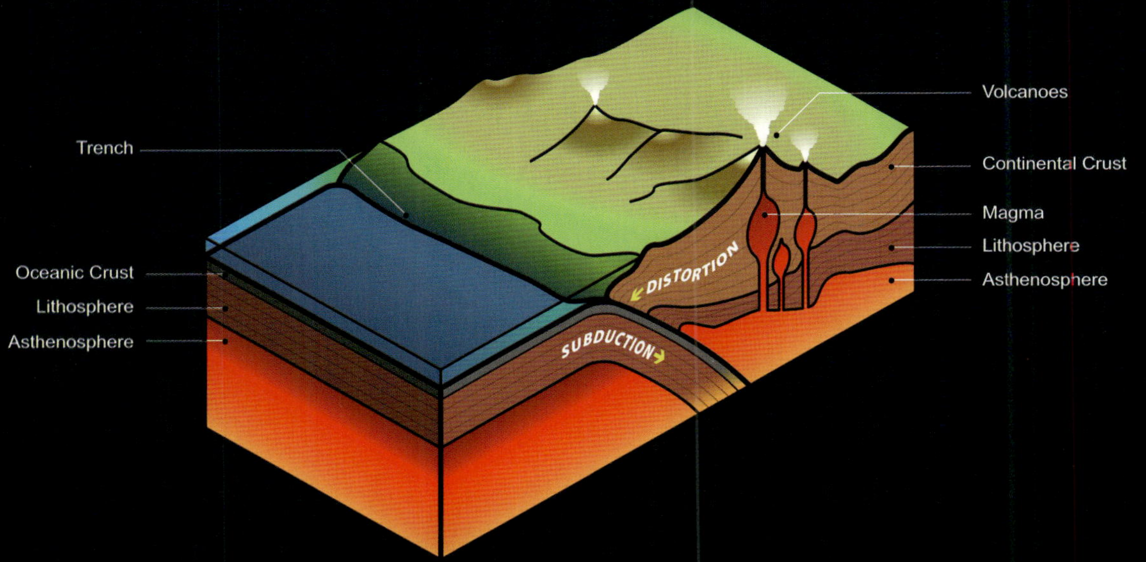

Trench
Oceanic Crust
Lithosphere
Asthenosphere
DISTORTION
SUBDUCTION
Volcanoes
Continental Crust
Magma
Lithosphere
Asthenosphere

20 **There are two different types of crust—continental and oceanic crust.** The continental crust makes up the land on the Earth. The oceanic crust forms the ocean. The continental crust is thicker than the oceanic crust.

INTRODUCTION

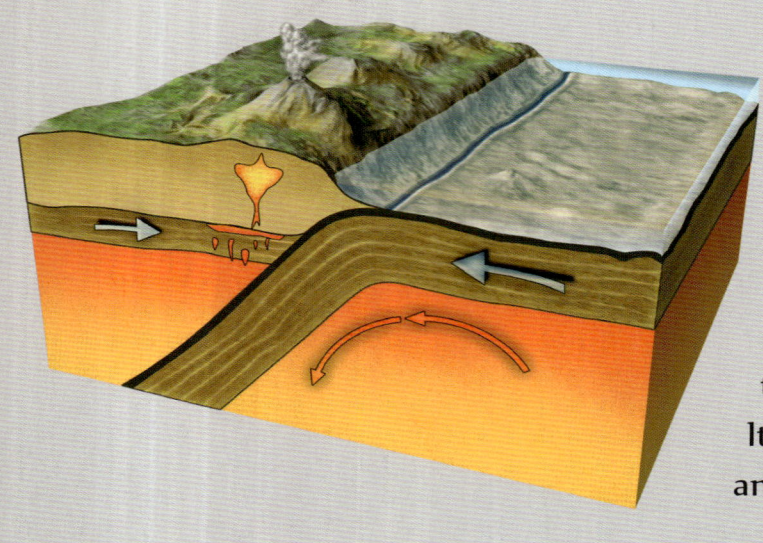

21 The continental crust is eight km to 70 km thick. Most of it is made of a type of rock called granite. The oceanic crust is thinner than the continental crust. It is about eight km thick and made mainly of basalt.

22 Did you know that the thinnest layer of the Earth is its crust? There are some areas of the Earth where the crust is so thin that hot magma (liquid rock) melts the rock above it and breaks through to the surface. These areas are called hot spots.

STRUCTURE OF EARTH

INTRODUCTION

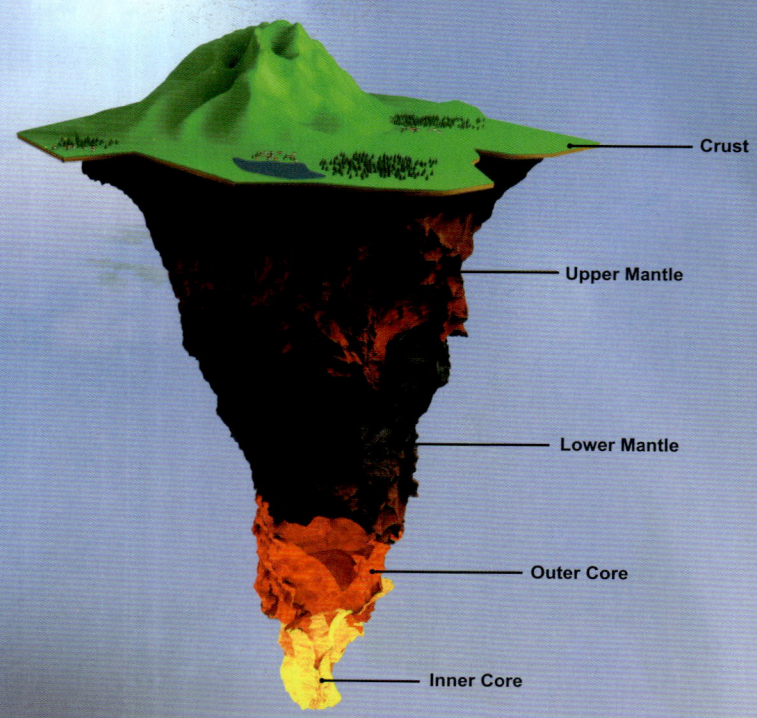

25 **The upper mantle is found approximately 670 km below the Earth's surface.** Due to extreme heat, the lower part of this layer comprises both solid and liquid rock. The upper portion is solid because of cooler temperatures.

26 **The Earth is surrounded by a layer of gases on all sides.** This layer is called the atmosphere. It comprises 78 per cent nitrogen, 21 per cent oxygen and many other gases in smaller quantities.

STRUCTURE OF EARTH

27 **The atmosphere is very essential for life on Earth.** It keeps the planet at a temperature suitable for living organisms. The ozone present in the Earth's atmosphere provides protection from harmful ultraviolet rays of the Sun. The oxygen is used by plants and animals to breathe.

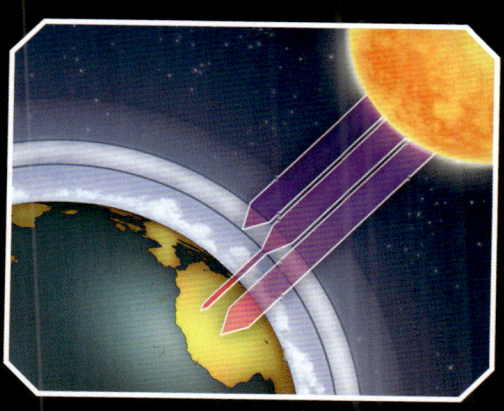

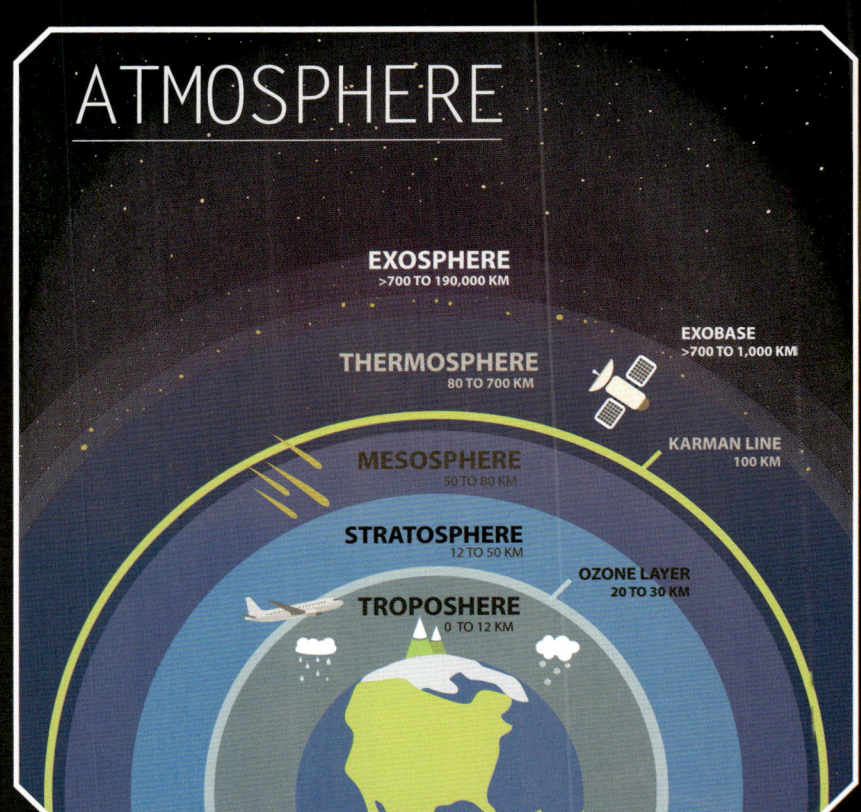

28 **The atmosphere begins from the Earth's surface and extends into space.** It is divided into many layers. The lowest layer of the Earth's atmosphere is called troposphere. It is about 16 cm thick.

INTRODUCTION

29 **The troposphere comprises the air we breathe.** It is the layer that supports life on Earth. Did you know that changes in weather take place when the troposphere gets heated by the rays of the Sun?

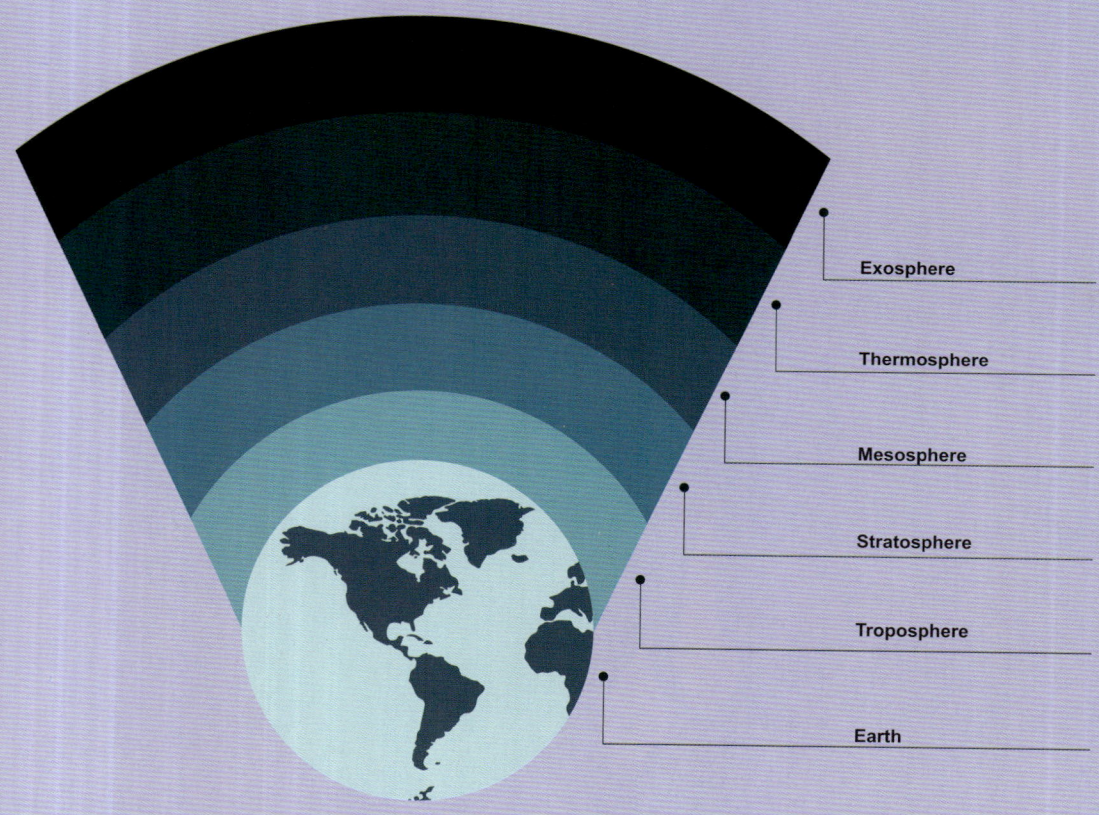

- Exosphere
- Thermosphere
- Mesosphere
- Stratosphere
- Troposphere
- Earth

30 **The layer above the troposphere is called stratosphere.** A common practice is to float special balloons filled with hydrogen or helium into the stratosphere. These balloons have devices that can send back useful information about weather conditions to scientists on the surface.

STRUCTURE OF EARTH

31 Beyond the stratosphere lies the thermosphere. From time to time, particles from the Sun are drawn into the Earth's atmosphere. This causes breathtaking lights called auroras to appear in the thermosphere near the North and South Poles.

32 The final and highest layer of the atmosphere is the exosphere. Beyond it is space. But there is no clear boundary to the outer edge of the atmosphere—it just fades into space.

INTRODUCTION

33 Man-made satellites orbit the Earth at a height of 160 km or higher from its surface, where the atmosphere is very thin. If they came any closer to the surface, the atmosphere would become dense. Then the satellites would have to push through layers of gas, which would slow them down and make them crash.

34 Satellites orbit the Earth from west to east over the equator. They move in the same direction and speed at which the Earth spins. Therefore, when viewed from Earth, these satellites do not appear to be moving.

Earth's Interior

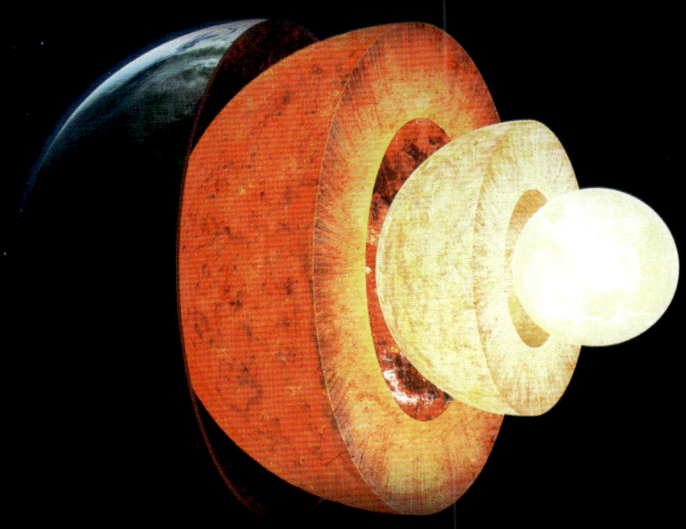

35 The Earth's centre comprises two layers—the outer core and the inner core. The outer core is the third layer of Earth (after the crust and mantle) and is made entirely of liquid.

36 Scientists believe that the composition of the Earth's core is similar to that of iron meteorites formed in the early solar system. The outer core is made of liquid iron and nickel, while the inner core comprises solid iron and nickel.

INTRODUCTION

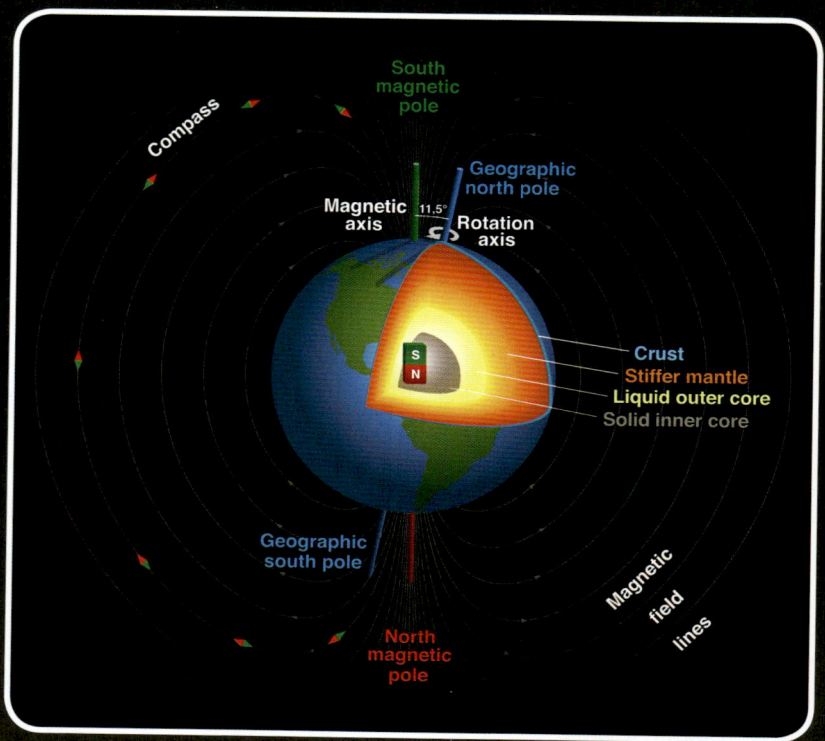

37 **The outer core is responsible for the Earth's magnetic field.** As the Earth spins on its axis, the iron inside the liquid outer core moves around. The movement in the liquid iron causes the development of powerful electric currents.

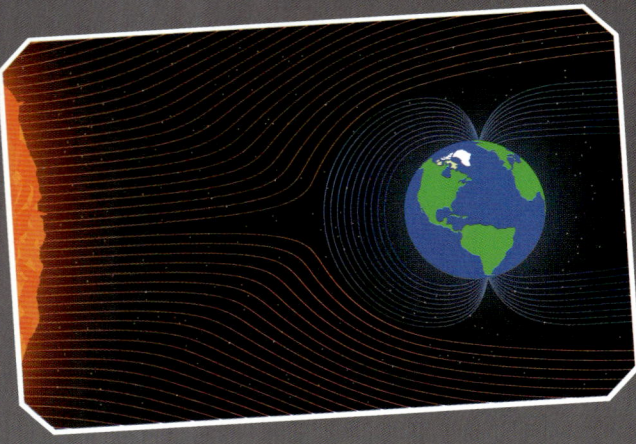

38 **These powerful currents cause invisible lines of force to stretch around the Earth, as well as thousands of kilometres into space, creating a magnetic field.** This magnetic field protects the Earth from harmful particles that come from the Sun.

EARTH'S INTERIOR

39
The inner core forms the fourth layer of the Earth. It is the hottest layer, with temperatures that reach incredible levels, ranging from 4,000–4,700°C (7,200–8,500°F).

40
Although the inner core is very hot, it is not liquid like the outer core. The inner core is a solid metallic ball made mainly of iron. It is solid due to the pressure caused by the weight of the Earth's other three layers upon it.

INTRODUCTION

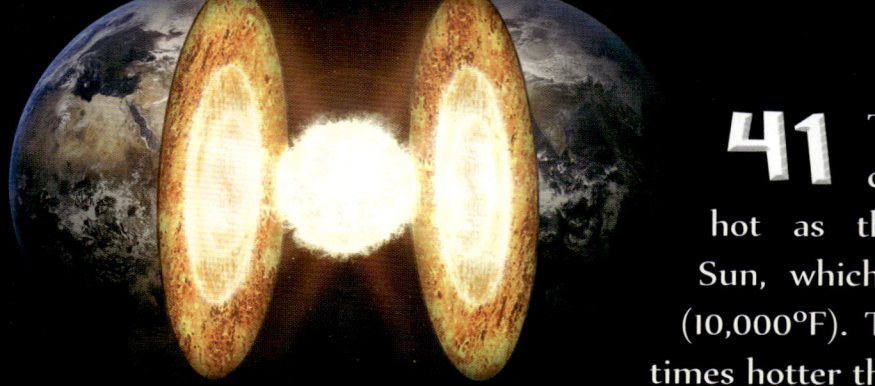

41 The Earth's inner core is as scorching hot as the surface of the Sun, which is about 5,500°C (10,000°F). That is about 6,000 times hotter than our atmosphere. That is enough heat to melt metals!

42 Sometimes hot molten rock, called magma, bursts through the Earth's surface in the form of a volcano. When magma erupts out of a volcano under immense pressure, it is called lava. Lava appears to be almost like a stream of fire.

EARTH'S INTERIOR

43 **Volcanic lava can be up to 12 times hotter than boiling water.** Did you know that volcanoes can be found on land, the ocean floor and even under ice, such as those found in Iceland?

44 **No man has ever ventured beyond the Earth's crust.** So how did scientists manage to find out so much about what lies inside our planet? The answer is seismic waves. These are waves caused by earthquakes and the movements of the oceans. Studying seismic waves can reveal a great deal about the Earth's interior.

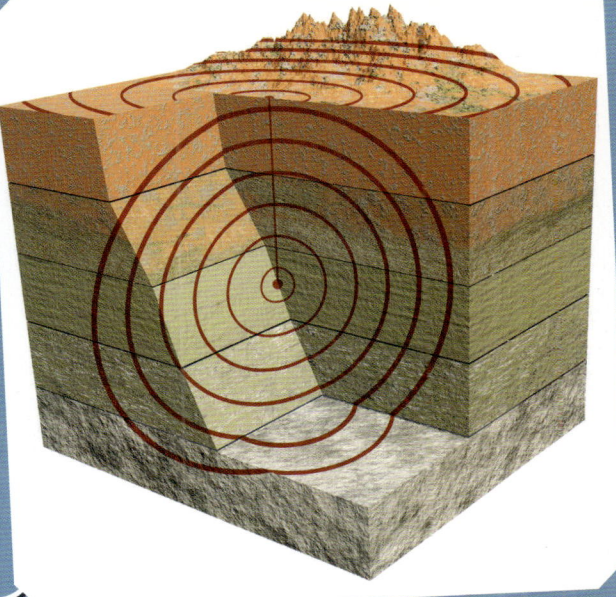

EARTH AND ITS CONSTITUENTS

The Beginning

45 You must have heard of Mars being called the 'Red Planet'. Similarly, the Earth is called the 'Blue Planet'. Astronauts have exclaimed that the planet appears to be blue from outer space. Even in the parts that are dark, facing away from the sun, astronauts can see millions of brilliant lights, thanks to the spread of electricity!

46 The land that we stand on is part of the solid crust on the surface of the Earth. This land above sea level only consists of about 30% of Earth's total area and is called the continental crust. It is generally older and thicker as compared to the oceanic crust.

THE BEGINNING

47 The Earth was formed millions of years ago and the scientists believe that it was nothing but a ball of gases and dust, floating in space. Can you imagine our planet in such a state? In fact, all the planets were formed through a gradual process of cooling down and solidification of gases. Did you know, several of the planets in the solar system are still largely in a gaseous form?

48 There are two theories regarding the formation of the Earth. One states that the materials stuck together and then separated to form the planet. The second theory states that the core was formed first and then the different surfaces gathered around it.

EARTH AND ITS CONSTITUENTS

49 Have you ever wondered how life came to exist on our planet? One of the major reasons for this was that Earth has the optimal atmospheric conditions that helped life to flourish here. This includes the right temperature, and the right mixture of gases in the atmosphere.

50 The other planets in the solar system also have atmospheres, but they do not support life forms. For example, Venus and Mars also have atmospheres of their own, but there is a greater concentration of gases such as sulphuric acid and carbon dioxide. Further, they are much closer to the Sun, and hence the temperatures are very high.

THE BEGINNING

51 **The atmosphere on the Earth is composed of a mixture of over 10 gases, which are collectively known as 'air'.** Apart from allowing us to breathe, the atmosphere also affects how we see the universe. It scatters the light coming from the Sun, making the sky appear blue.

52 **Did you know that the Earth is the only planet which is not named after a deity?** All the other planets in our Solar System are named after Roman gods and goddesses.

EARTH AND ITS CONSTITUENTS

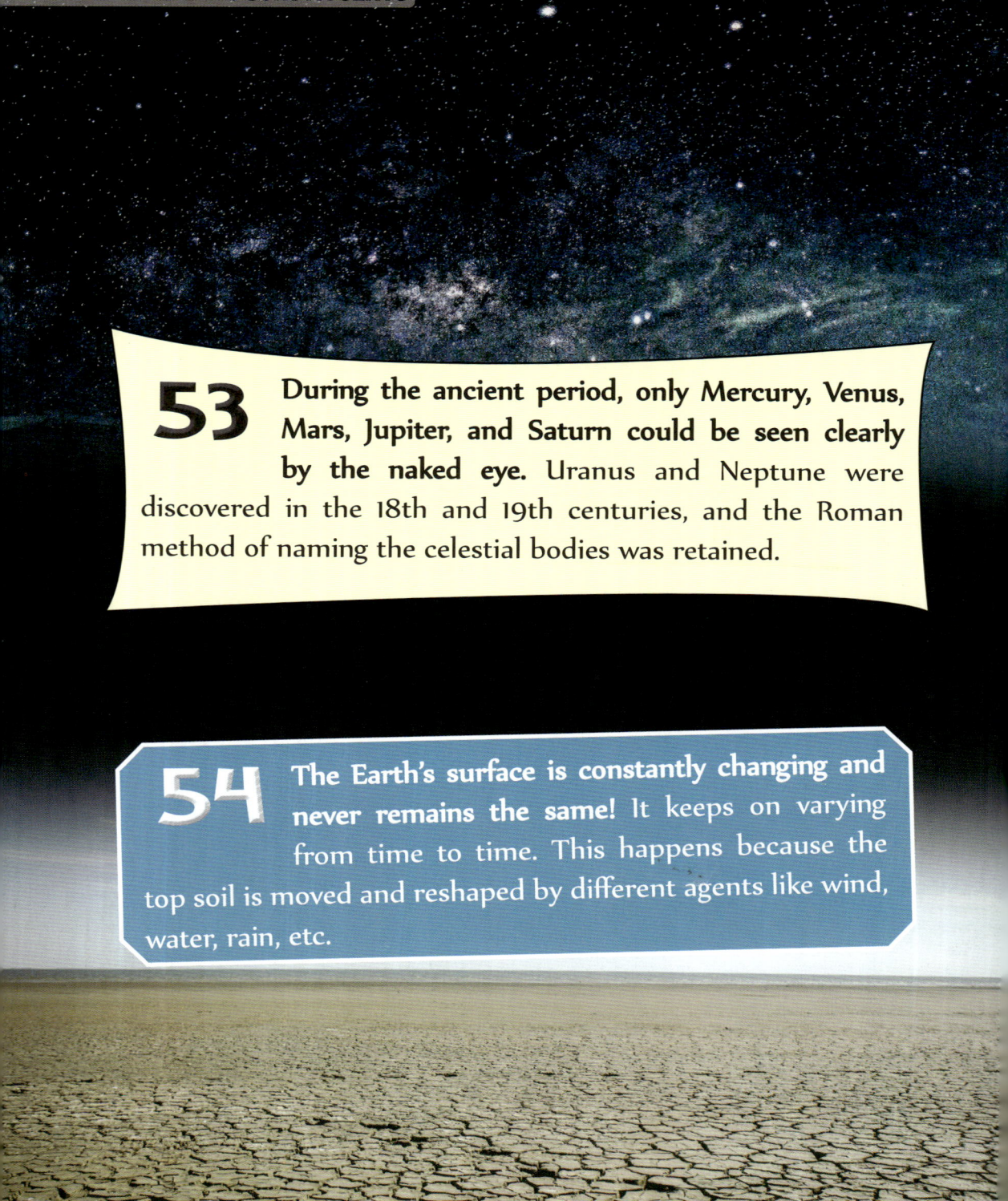

53 During the ancient period, only Mercury, Venus, Mars, Jupiter, and Saturn could be seen clearly by the naked eye. Uranus and Neptune were discovered in the 18th and 19th centuries, and the Roman method of naming the celestial bodies was retained.

54 The Earth's surface is constantly changing and never remains the same! It keeps on varying from time to time. This happens because the top soil is moved and reshaped by different agents like wind, water, rain, etc.

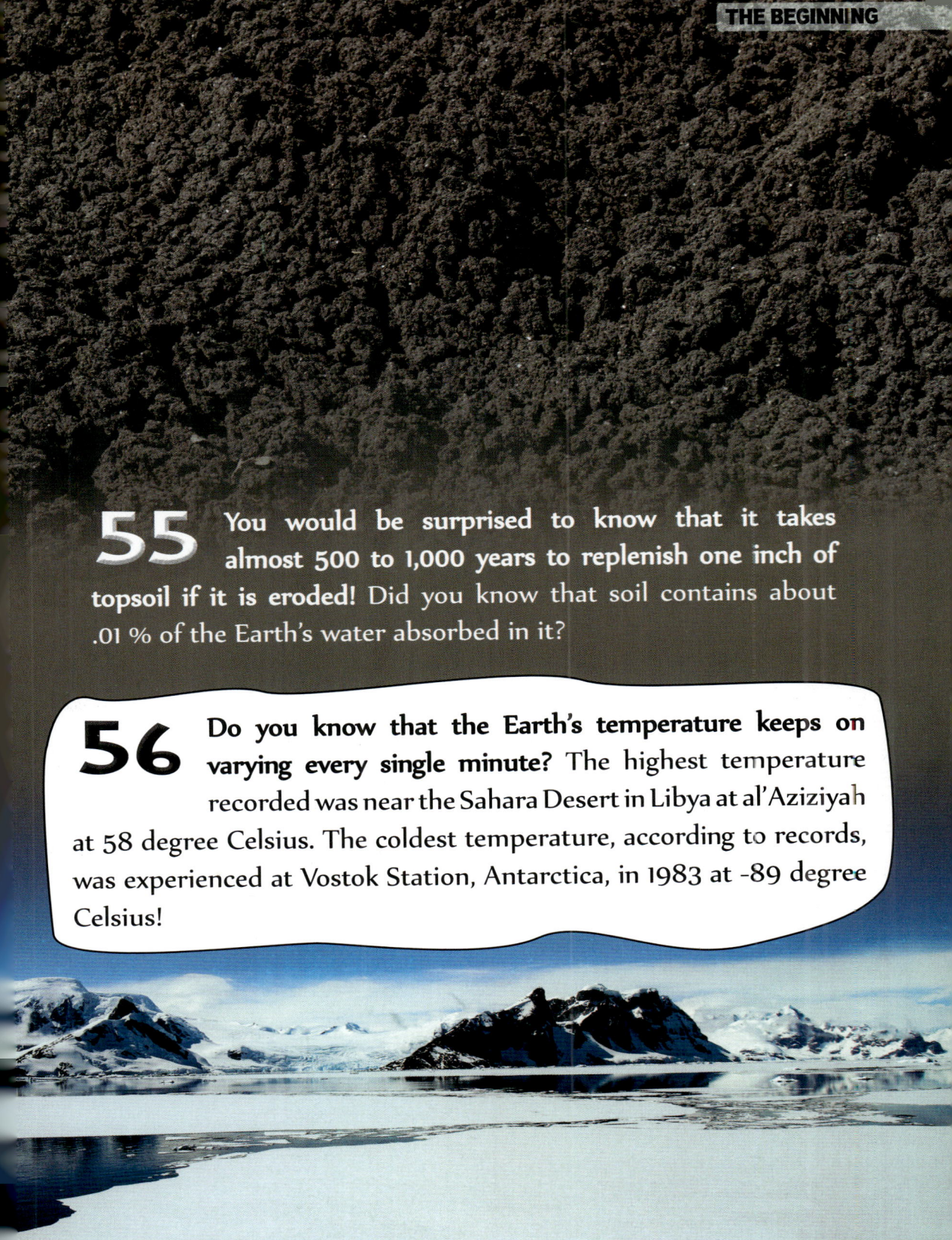

55 **You would be surprised to know that it takes almost 500 to 1,000 years to replenish one inch of topsoil if it is eroded!** Did you know that soil contains about .01 % of the Earth's water absorbed in it?

56 **Do you know that the Earth's temperature keeps on varying every single minute?** The highest temperature recorded was near the Sahara Desert in Libya at al'Aziziyah at 58 degree Celsius. The coldest temperature, according to records, was experienced at Vostok Station, Antarctica, in 1983 at -89 degree Celsius!

EARTH AND ITS CONSTITUENTS

57 Did you know that the Earth's crust is not stable? Though it appears to be strong and solid-looking, it is extremely changeable. Just beneath the crust, that we can see, lie a series of moving, shifting tectonic plates. The movement of these plates causes changes on the Earth's crust.

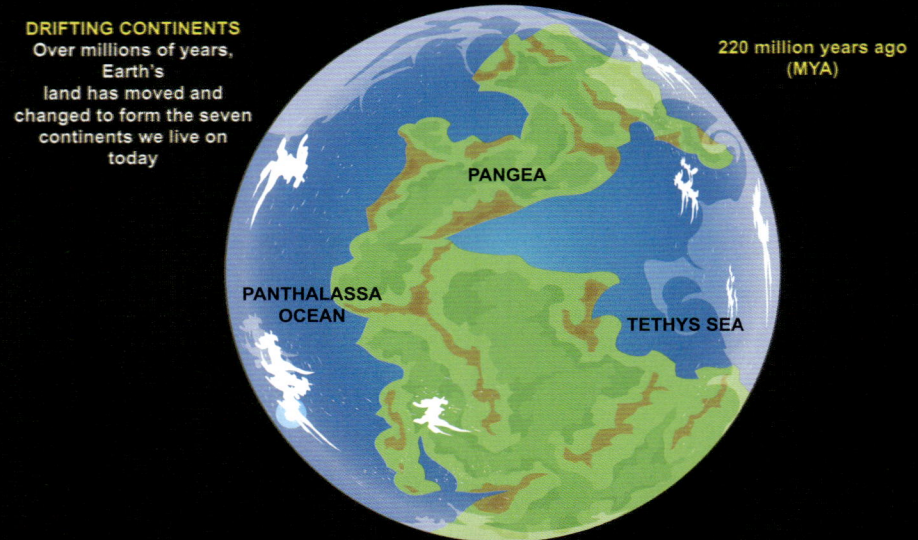

DRIFTING CONTINENTS
Over millions of years, Earth's land has moved and changed to form the seven continents we live on today

220 million years ago (MYA)

PANGEA

PANTHALASSA OCEAN

TETHYS SEA

58 Millions of years ago, Earth had a completely different appearance. As you know, the continents were all clustered together and formed one huge continent known as Pangaea. Did you know that geologists believe that our continents are still drifting even today? This means that over time, the face of the Earth could change completely once again!

EARTH'S SEASONS

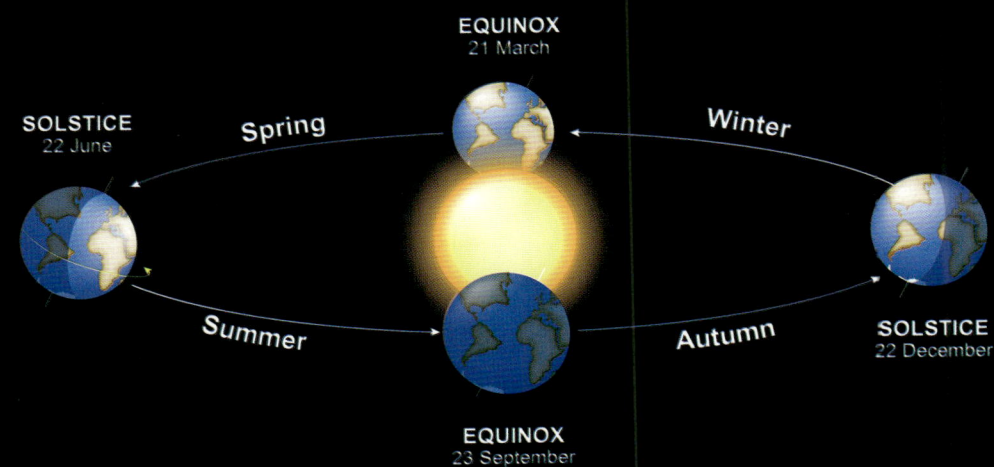

59 Did you know that the Earth has one of the most circular orbits of all the planets in the solar system? Its axis of rotation is tilted 23.4° away from the right angle of its orbital plane. This factor also results in the varying seasons we experience on the Earth.

60 The Earth was formed roughly 4.54 billion years ago. This planet has unique features which are not found in any other planet in our Solar System. However, by studying the Earth, we can try to learn and understand the phenomenon that take place on the other planets as well.

EARTH AND ITS CONSTITUENTS

61 **Did you know that the Earth is recycled constantly?** The Earth's rock cycle transforms igneous rocks to sedimentary rocks to metamorphic rocks and back again. The leftovers, which are rich in carbons, are carried into the interior of the Earth and recycled into molten magma!

62 **Do you know that Earth was once believed to be the centre of the Universe?** Ancient astronomers believed that the Earth was fixed and other celestial bodies, including the Sun, travelled in circular orbits around it.

63 **Do you know the first life-form that developed on Earth?** It is believed that life first developed in the oceans by a process called abiodenesis or biopoiesis. This is a natural process in which life grows from non-living matter like simple organic compounds, bacteria or fungi.

Fossils

64 Scientists learn a lot about the past of the Earth, and its organisms through a study of fossils. However, the traces of fossils are not always the original parts of creatures. Often, they are just marks or impressions which were made by them upon the soil or rock.

EARTH AND ITS CONSTITUENTS

65 **Do you know what coprolites are?** The ancient dung which is preserved as fossils is called 'coprolites' by geologists! Fossils are often found in groups, and single fossils are rare. Depending on what kind of fossils are found, we can learn about many different facets of life in the past.

66 **The word 'fossil' comes from a Latin word which means 'dug up'.** Usually fossils were created when the remains were covered by soil and rocks, and then intense pressure caused the debris to become packed and hard. The soil often turned into sedimentary rock over time, and this is also why fossils are usually found in sedimentary rocks!

FOSSILS

67 Fossil fuels are created by the action of intense heat and pressure on buried plant and animal matter over a long period of time. Fossil fuels such as coal and petroleum are a reservoir of energy, and have been burnt by humans for heat and light for thousands of years.

68 Burning of fossil fuels is one of the major causes for emission of carbon dioxide in the atmosphere. This leads to the greenhouse effect and causes global warming. This is why scientists are now searching for other sources of energy, like solar energy and wind energy.

EARTH AND ITS CONSTITUENTS

69 **Did you know that usually a fossil is not complete?** In other words, sometimes only a small part of an organism may survive as a fossil, such as dinosaur bones. In the case of impression fossils, such as footprints, too, we may find a few prints from which we can deduce and learn as much as possible.

70 **What is palaeontology?** It is the branch of biology which tells us about the different forms of life which existed in the ancient periods by studying fossils. There are many kinds of fossils we can study today, based on different ways of fossil preservation.

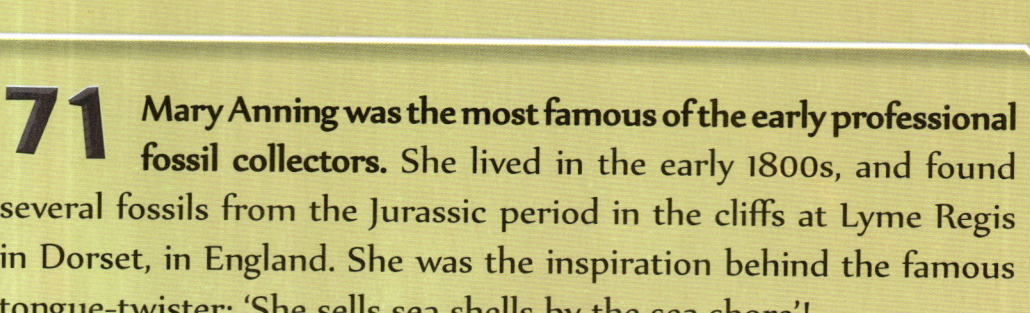

71 **Mary Anning was the most famous of the early professional fossil collectors.** She lived in the early 1800s, and found several fossils from the Jurassic period in the cliffs at Lyme Regis in Dorset, in England. She was the inspiration behind the famous tongue-twister: 'She sells sea shells by the sea shore'!

72 **Do you know what Trilobites are?** They were a class of early arthropods that lived in oceans and seas throughout the world. They existed approximately 450 million years ago, at the beginning of the Palaeozoic Era.

73 **Trilobite fossils have been found on every single continent.** Trilobite fossils are very useful for scientists, as they can see the subtle evolutionary changes that took place over time through the various fossils.

74 **Did you know that sometimes fossils of marine animals are found buried inside sedimentary rocks far inland?** Just like creatures on land, creatures underwater too get buried under silt and mud, and over time they become fossilized. However, due to the tectonic forces, over the centuries, some of the land that was once underwater has now risen and become part of the dry land!

EARTH AND ITS CONSTITUENTS

75 **Do you know why fossils are useful?** As you can guess, we can learn about the various prehistoric creatures and their environment. We can also learn a lot about the process of evolution. We can even use fossils to date sedimentary rocks, and tectonic movements!

76 **There are two important types of fossils: mold fossils and petrified fossils.** Usually, mold fossils are formed when the living organism is trapped in sediments which later become bedrock. As time passes, the organism decays, leaving behind a gap between the sediment. Over time, minerals from the surrounding sediment and from the rock seep into the gap between the rocks, creating a hard fossil.

77 **Ginkgo Biloba is a native plant of China and has no living relatives.** In the sedimentary rocks of the Jurassic period, the fossilized imprints of the leaf of this tree dating back to 135 to 210 million years were found. The extract of this tree is today used to improve memory and concentration power.

78 **Have you heard of the index fossils?** These are the fossils of organisms which scientists use to predict how old the layers of rock are. As you may know, sedimentary rock is formed in layers. Thus, by examining which layer the fossil was found in, and comparing it with other fossils and rock samples, it is possible to understand more about the formation of the Earth's current crust.

79 **Not every fossil can be an index fossil.** To act as an index fossil, the organisms must be easy to identify, must have lived for only a short period of time and must be common in rocks from most of the world.

EARTH AND ITS CONSTITUENTS

80 **Almost 95% of all living animals present on the Earth are invertebrates.** Do you know that most of the fossils we have found are of invertebrates, or animals without bones?

81 **Did you know that Cyanobacteria are the oldest fossils present on the Earth?** Some of the oldest of these are the fossils dating back to 3.5 billion years from Western Australia. These micro-fossils are easy to recognise, as these are unicellular bacteria without a nucleus and have hardly changed over time.

82 **Fossils have been called the footprints of the past.** But did you know that actual fossilised footprints and other such impressions are known as trace fossils? These are the remains that we study where only the traces of a living organism are left. For example, it could be a footprint, eggs, leaves, or even a burrow!

FOSSILS

83 Horseshoe crabs are called living fossils. Their fossils have been uncovered, dating back to about 450 million years, and the creatures are still found roaming around muddy oceans. These are closely associated with arachnids like spiders and scorpions. Unfortunately, they are decreasing in number due to habitat destruction.

84 Did you know that the oldest fish fossil recorded was found at Chengjiang in the Yunnan Province of China? The site has a vast variety of marine fossils from the Cambrian period, about 530 million years ago. Scientists say that this was the period when several of the species we see today first emerged.

EARTH AND ITS CONSTITUENTS

85 On Earth, shark fossils dating back about 450 million years have been found. Two such species are the goblin shark and frilled shark. The goblin shark was first seen in 1898 at the coast of Japan. They grow 10 to 13 feet in length and are known as 'vampire sharks', as they hate sunlight.

86 Ctenophores are living fossils. They are often referred to as comb jelly, because they have cilia that look like rows of comb teeth. They are hermaphrodites, and a single organism can fertilize its own eggs, without a mate. Similar fossils have been found dating to at least 600 million years ago!

Soil

87 Soil is one of the most important parts of our living environment on the Earth. It supports a number of ecosystems and organisms. However, soil is at the bottom of the food chain, even though it is the cornerstone of life on Earth!

88 The colour, nutrient composition and texture of the soil vary from place to place and time to time. The proportion of sand, clay and silt mixed together give different soil types their distinct textures. Most soils are a mixture of these three components.

89 If you were to grab a handful of soil, what would you see? Soil is composed of pebbles and rocky material of different sizes, minerals, and remains of dead animals and plants. It also includes living matter, such as insects and worms.

EARTH AND ITS CONSTITUENTS

90 **Soil varies from place to place, region to region and time to time.** Thus, the soil in a desert is very different from the one found in a river delta. But it is very interesting to learn that the soil layer of Earth is constantly in motion. For instance, on the slopes of hills, soil moves down slowly, in a process known as 'soil creep'.

91 **Do you know how soil is formed?** Often, rocks are broken up by different agents like ice, frost, wind and water. The smaller particles that are formed by this process, come together to create soil. This loose soil is held together by moisture. The roots of plants can further bind it together.

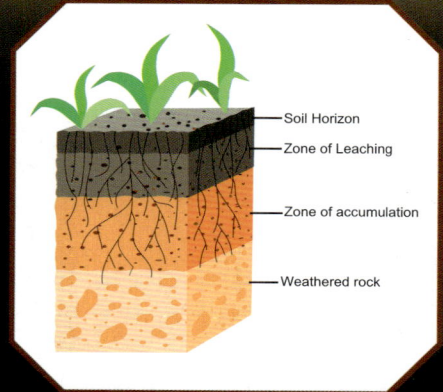

92 **When plants die, they add to the richness of the soil.** This is because the dead plant material starts to decompose, and gradually merges into the soil, fertilising it. Soil takes many years to form and replenish, but can be easily destroyed by human actions, such as bad farming methods.

93 **Soil plays the role of a filter and cleans underground water.** It is home to thousands of microorganisms that help in maintaining soil fertility. This, in turn, helps to support plant life.

94 **Soil comprises 45% minerals, 25% water, 25% air and 5% organic matter.** Geologists, who study soil, have identified six layers within it, known as horizons. These are horizons O, A, E, B, C and R.

95 **Soil is an essential, non-renewable source.** Soil is polluted on a large scale by industries, planters, etc. When large amounts of industrial waste and chemicals are dumped on and absorbed by the soil, its nutritive values are reduced. This makes soil unfit for growth of plants and trees, and becomes barren.

EARTH AND ITS CONSTITUENTS

96 Soil is a very important natural resource also as a **source for minerals.** It is thus used for making medicines, utensils, and other goods. Soil is very precious. Hence, it must be conserved by preventing soil erosion and pollution.

97 Did you know that the colour of soil varies from layer to layer? Soil occupies 25% of the Earth's surface, and about 10% of soil is used to grow food. Thus, it is important to keep soil healthy, as it affects the health of people, plants and animals.

98 **Soil erosion is caused due to different reasons.** Some of these include: erosion due to constant and forceful flowing water, blowing of wind at high speeds, gradual erosion through glaciers and ice, over-grazing of animals, high temperature and rate of precipitation, etc.

SOIL

99 **Living things play a vital role in replenishing the nutrients of the soil.** When plants and animals die, their left-over body is broken down by creatures like beetles, microscopic bacteria and fungi. This results in release of minerals into the soil. The minerals fertilise plants and the cycle of life begins again.

100 **Soil must be conserved and protected to meet the future demands of mankind.** The practice of conservation methods, such as terrace farming, contour farming, restoration of wetlands, and afforestation, can help to protect soil.

101 **Plants absorb nitrogen directly from the soil.** Nitrogen is an important component for all living things. The nitrogen cycle shows how nitrogen moves through different elements, including the atmosphere and the soil. There are different steps in the nitrogen cycle—fixation, nitrification, assimilation, ammonification and denitrification.

Weather

102 **Weather plays an important role in everyone's life.** The average weather of a particular place or region over a few years is known as climate. It can be briefly described as hot, dry, cold, windy, wet or rainy.

103 **Weather depicts the condition of the atmosphere of an area at a given time.** The weather refers to the everyday conditions, while climate refers to an average over time. Weather is thus a short-term situation, whereas climate is a long-term characteristic of an area.

104 The climate of a place depends on its location on the Earth's surface, and the intensity of the sun's rays received there. Other important factors that significantly influence climate are distance from the equator, oceanic currents and distance from the sea.

21st March beginning of spiring

21st June beginning of summer

22nd December beginning of winter

23rd September beginning of autumn

105 Some areas which are small in size have their own climatic conditions, known as 'microclimate'. This usually is significantly different from the climate of the surrounding areas. For instance, valleys often have a completely different, milder climate than the surrounding high mountains.

106 The Sun is a big ball of a variety of super-hot gases. It provides us with both heat and sunlight. The heat of the Sun is a major factor that ensures favourable or fair weather conditions. Sunlight heats up air, and the hot air rises. This movement of air creates wind and affects the climate. Thus, changes in solar output also affect our climate both directly and indirectly.

53

EARTH AND ITS CONSTITUENTS

107 Rainbows are formed when the Sun shines through tiny, fragmented raindrops, which refract the light and split it into seven colours. Rainbows are actually complete circles, but we can see only a part of it.

108 For centuries, humans have used the clouds as a method of predicting the weather. For instance, rainclouds are dark and low, indicating imminent precipitation. On the other hand, fluffy cumulus clouds indicate clear, fair weather.

WEATHER

109 There are mainly three types of clouds. Cumulus clouds are also known as 'cauliflower clouds' because of their shape. Cirrus clouds are feathery and form a layer of white clouds in the sky. They are usually found around 20,000 feet high in the sky. Stratus clouds are layered and often seen in hilly areas.

110 When the temperature is below freezing point and water vapours turn into ice, this forms frost. One type of frost is 'hoar frost', which covers the ground and is so white in colour that it appears like snow. This occurs when the sky is clear without clouds.

111 We all know that water is an essential component of life on the Earth. Rain is one of the most important methods by which water is cycled over the Earth. Rain is beneficial when it falls in an appropriate quantity, because excess of rain can cause floods and damage to life and property, while lack of rain can cause droughts and people can die of hunger.

EARTH AND ITS CONSTITUENTS

112 Falling of water in its various forms—as water, hail, or snow—from clouds is known as **precipitation.** Small drops of rain are known as drizzling drops. Did you know that rainfall is the purest form of naturally occurring water on the Earth?

113 Wind has a very strong and powerful effect on the lives of human beings. The first trial to know more about the characteristics of wind was made by Rear Admiral Sir Francis Beaufort in 1805. He made a scale for sailors to measure the wind strength at sea.

114 Wind is the movement of air, and it carries immense energy. In the past, wind energy was used to grind grain, through small windmills. Now, it is also used to generate electricity with the help of large wind turbines.

WEATHER

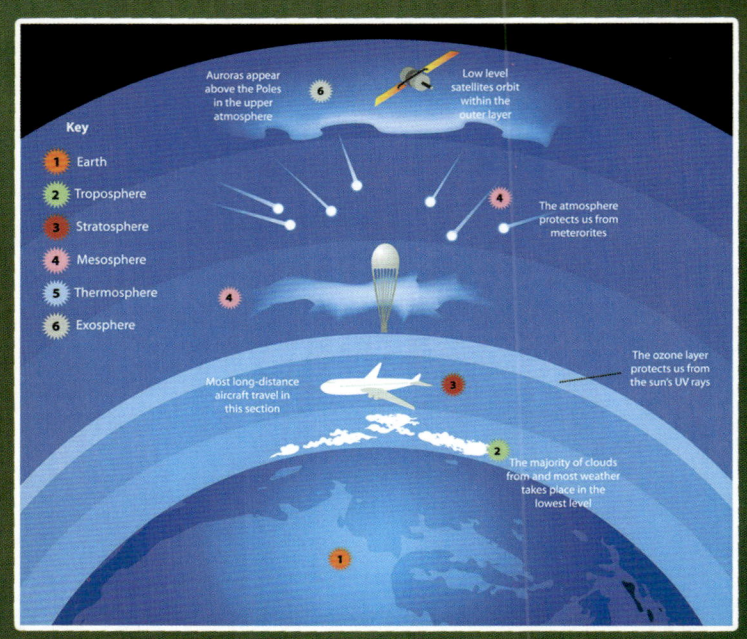

115 **The atmosphere is not just a standard body of air.** It is denser near the Earth's surface, and much less dense the further up we go. Most of the weather activities happen in the troposphere which is located nearest to the surface. It is followed by the stratosphere. The outermost layer is called the exosphere.

116 **Do you know how hailstones are formed?** The formation of hailstones depends on the temperature of air in the clouds. They are formed when heavy currents flow inside the clouds. Hail can cause severe damages, for instance, it can damage fruits, break window, dent cars, and even hurt humans and animals.

Environment

117 We all know that the Earth has been in existence for a very long time, but did you know that the Earth's environment has not remained the same? These changes took place as a result of natural forces. In recent years, humans have also caused great damage to the environment.

118 The environment comprises all the living organisms and all the forces of nature which surround us. Thus, the atmosphere, weather, plant life, animals, as well as human activity, all come together to create the environment.

119 An ecosystem is an interconnected community of living creatures and the environment around them. For example, a rainforest is a different ecosystem from a desert. Pollution in the ecosystem can cause the living organisms that live there to suffer. It may even lead to extinction of species.

ENVIRONMENT

120 Do you know why governments today often ban the use of plastic bags? Plastic is not biodegradable. It is believed that plastic bags which end up in the ocean are responsible for killing approximately 1 million sea creatures every year!

121 We know that the Earth is covered by land and water. But did you know that even the atmosphere has water? You would be surprised to know that there is more water present in the form of vapour, than in all the rivers on the Earth measured collectively!

122 Plastic is a synthetic material, usually made from petrochemicals. Have you ever wondered what happens to all the plastic bottles we throw away? It is important to recycle plastic bottles. If you do not recycle them, then it would take thousands of years for a bottle to decompose.

EARTH AND ITS CONSTITUENTS

123 One of the most important mantras in the modern age is 'Reduce, Reuse, Recycle'. This means we must use what can be used again, reduce our dependence on new plastic products, and recycle old plastics. This will help to safeguard the Earth from further destruction.

124 There are very few places on the Earth that are not polluted today. Did you know that Antarctica is protected by anti-pollution laws? This has helped it remain one of the cleanest places.

125 Did you know that the pollution in one country can cause damage to the environment of other countries as well? For example, pollution in China can affect the environment of Peru.

ENVIRONMENT

126 Vehicles emit polluting gases into the atmosphere. Carpooling can help reduce this kind of pollution and it is also effective in saving money. More people should carpool together.

127 **The natural environment is the one which occurs naturally, without any alterations.** However, in the modern world, most of it has been converted into human environment, as we have cut down trees, built structures, paved roads, etc. There are hardly any places left on the planet that still have their natural environment intact.

Water Bodies

128 We all know that approximately 70% of the Earth's surface is covered with water. Did you know that the tides which are formed in the oceans are caused by the rotation of the Earth? The gravity of the Moon and the Sun are responsible for pulling the water towards them while the Earth moves, and hence the tides are formed.

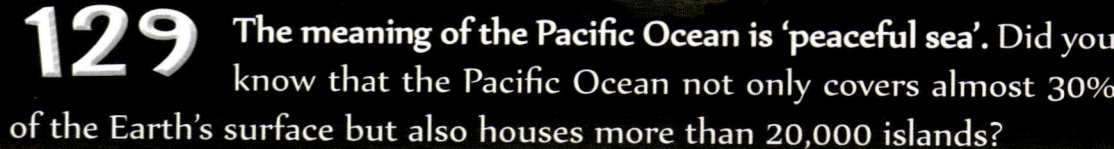

129 The meaning of the Pacific Ocean is 'peaceful sea'. Did you know that the Pacific Ocean not only covers almost 30% of the Earth's surface but also houses more than 20,000 islands?

130 Even the landmasses on Earth have water sources flowing over them. These are the rivers, which provide water inland. The longest river in the world is the Nile River, while the second longest is the Amazon River.

WATER BODIES

131 **The waste that is dumped into the water bodies ends up polluting them.** Did you know that the Ganges, Yangtze and Indus rivers are some of the most polluted rivers in the world?

132 Did you know that the deepest point on Earth is Mariana Trench at 36,198 feet? It is located in the Pacific Ocean. The deeper you go, the greater the pressure underwater. Humans cannot survive in such pressure conditions. Yet, there are unique marine creatures who thrive in this kind of an environment.

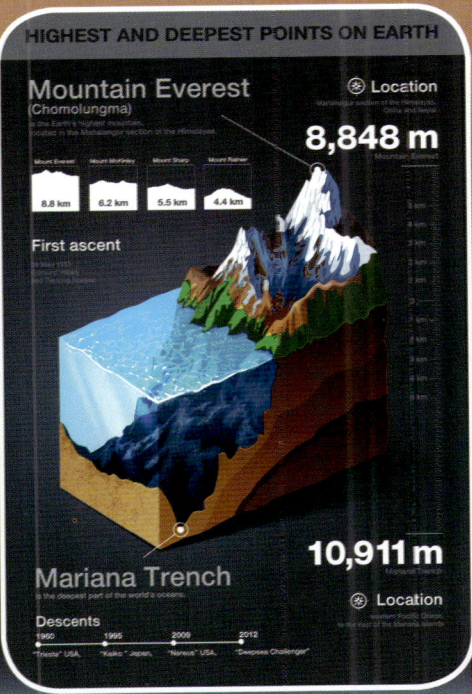

133 **The midpoint between the North and South Poles is signified by an imaginary line known as the Equator.** Did you know that if we take the entire coastline of all the landmasses and combine them, then we can cover the Equator almost 12 times?

EARTH AND ITS CONSTITUENTS

134 **Of all the oceans, the Arctic Ocean is the smallest one.** Most of it is present in the form of solid ice, as the temperatures at the Pole are very low.

135 **Coral reefs are a unique and important ecosystem within the oceans.** However, more than 50% of the reefs in the world are in danger of getting destroyed because of the pollution spread by humans.

136 **In Central Asia, there is an inland sea called the Aral Sea.** At present, it is only 10% of what it used to be, after the engineers of the Soviet era diverted its water elsewhere for cotton cultivation. This is how human actions harm the environment.

WATER BODIES

137 **Did you know that the Baltic Sea and the North Sea which share a border do not mix with one another?** The reason behind this phenomena is the difference in density of both the seas.

138 **All across the world gold is known to be a precious metal, which is very expensive.** But it is interesting to learn that there is so much gold in the oceans that if it were extracted, everyone would become rich!

139 **Did you know that we have not yet explored the majority of what the oceans have to offer?** Humans have more knowledge of the surface of the planet Mars than of the Earth's oceans!

EARTH AND ITS CONSTITUENTS

140 We know that there are underwater volcanoes and islands, but did you know that there are underwater lakes, rivers, and waterfalls? The lakes are mainly formed when the salt which dissolves in that portion of water makes them denser and heavier than the rest of the water.

141 Did you know that the sea levels have increased by 10-25 cm on an average in the last century? This is because the rising temperatures in the world are gradually melting the polar ice. The scientists predict that sea levels could rise further, making coastal areas go underwater.

WATER BODIES

142 Countries that are along the coast of oceans conduct almost 90% of their trade through sea and ocean routes. Did you know that many nations make use of underwater cables to establish contact with each other?

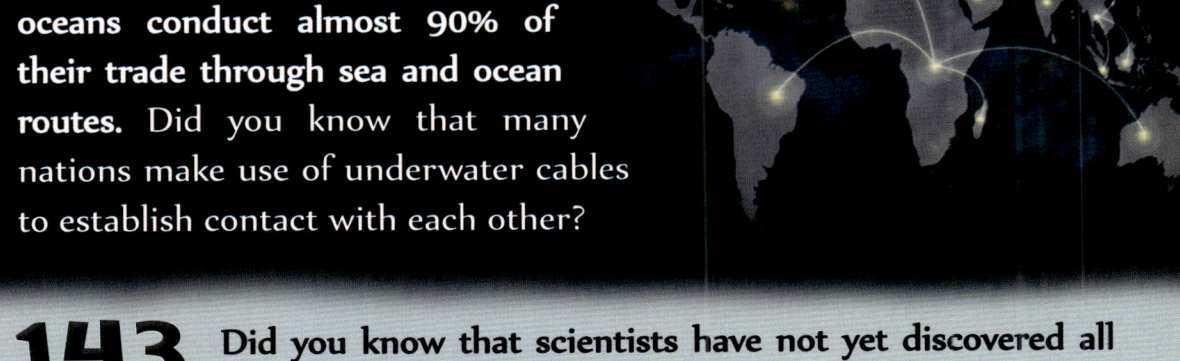

143 Did you know that scientists have not yet discovered all the species of living things in the oceans? There are still thousands of species which are unknown to us.

144 We all know how humans have polluted the land and water bodies like lakes and rivers. But did you know, even the vast oceans have been polluted? There is an oceanic gyre or vortex which contains marine debris and other polluting substances, and is known as the Great Pacific Garbage patch.

PHYSICAL GEOGRAPHY

Earth's Atmosphere

145 **The Earth's unique atmosphere is the reason that life can survive on it.** The atmosphere is made of layers of gases that envelop the whole planet. It protects us from the Sun's harmful rays, retains heat and keeps a temperature balance on Earth.

146 **The atmosphere is bound to the Earth by gravity.** The Earth's gravity determines the thickness of its atmosphere. Since gravity depends on mass, a planet with higher mass will have a thicker atmosphere. The Earth's atmosphere is around 480 km thick.

147 **The Earth's atmosphere mainly comprises nitrogen and oxygen.** Two gases, argon and carbon dioxide, amount to just around 1 per cent. There are also trace amounts of other gases and water vapour.

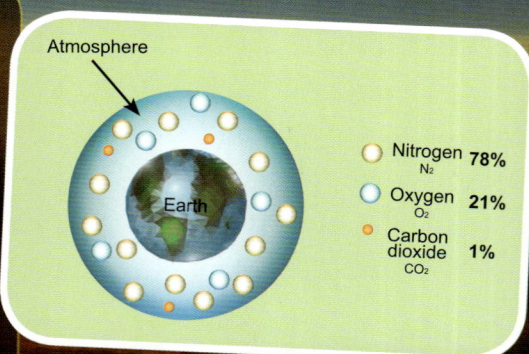

EARTH'S ATMOSPHERE

148 The density of the atmosphere varies at different points. As one travels upwards, its density becomes thinner. Based on its density, scientists have divided the atmosphere into five layers — troposphere, stratosphere, mesosphere, thermosphere and exosphere.

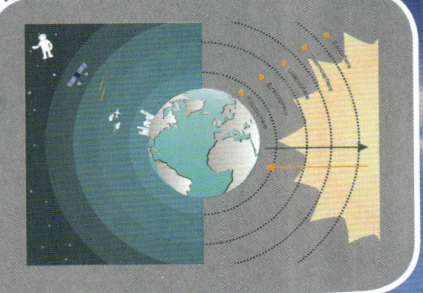

149 Closest to the Earth's surface is the troposphere. Extending from seven to 20 km, the troposphere is the thickest layer, containing half of the planet's atmosphere. This layer also contains water vapour and dust. Hence, this is where we find clouds.

150 The second layer is the stratosphere. Starting above the troposphere, it extends up to 50 km above ground. The most important component here is ozone, which absorbs the Sun's harmful radiation. The atmosphere here is dry and very thin.

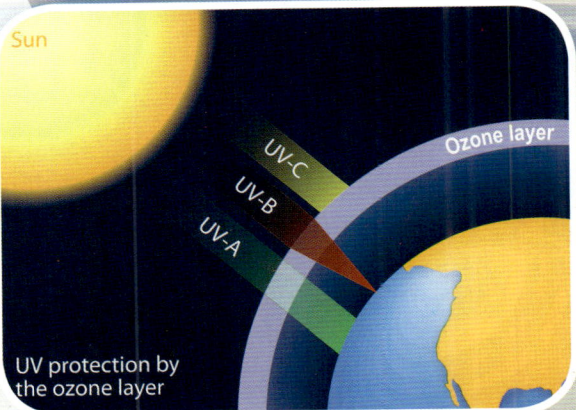

UV protection by the ozone layer

PHYSICAL GEOGRAPHY

151 **Above the stratosphere is the mesosphere, extending from 50 km to 85 km above ground.** The topmost part of this layer, known as mesopause, is the coldest part of Earth's atmosphere. It is here that meteors burn up when they enter Earth's atmosphere.

152 **The fourth layer, just above the mesosphere, is the thermosphere.** It extends from 90 km up to 1,000 km. The density here is very low and temperatures can reach 1,500 degree Celsius.. This thin layer is where we will find many of our space shuttles, as well as the International Space Station.

153 **The thermosphere is also the site for the most spectacular natural fireworks display — the auroras at the North and South Pole.** When charged particles from the Sun's rays collide with air particles in the thermosphere, we get colourful emissions of light called auroras.

EARTH'S ATMOSPHERE

154 The fifth and final layer is the exosphere where the atmosphere merges into outer space. This thin layer has widely spread hydrogen and helium particles. The particles here constantly interact with outer space and often escape into it.

155 The pollution on the Earth is changing our atmosphere in many ways, for instance, by depleting the ozone layer in the stratosphere. Scientists have found holes in the ozone layer. As a result of this, harmful UV rays can now reach the Earth's surface and cause diseases like skin cancer.

156 We experience the atmosphere in the form of weather and climate. Weather is the condition of the atmosphere during a short span of time. It can change from minute-to-minute. For example, you may wake up to sunny weather, which suddenly turns windy.

PHYSICAL GEOGRAPHY

157 **Climate indicates the usual atmospheric conditions in a place, such as dryness, humidity or wind.** The difference between weather and climate is that while weather refers to atmospheric conditions over a short span of time, climate is determined by the average behaviour of atmospheric conditions over a longer period of time.

158 **Meteorologists are scientists who study atmospheric patterns and predict weather conditions.** They use different tools like thermometer, barometer, anemometers and radars to predict weather conditions like rain, thunderstorm, hurricanes and even drought.

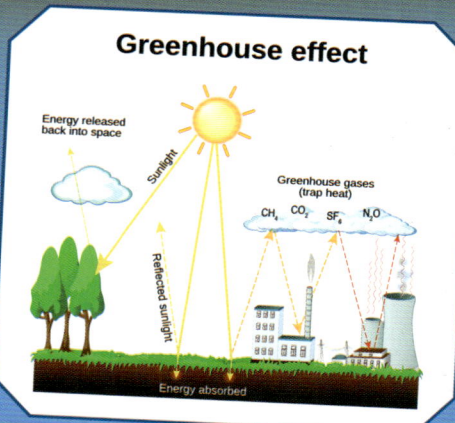

159 **The average of the regional climates forms Earth's global climate.** Meteorological data shows that the global climate is slowly becoming warmer. Scientists believe that an increase in gases, like carbon dioxide in the air traps heat within the atmosphere.

Moving Continents

160 Earth has not always been as we see it today. In fact, its surface is always changing. The shape and position of continents is constantly evolving. This change is so slow that we do not even notice it.

161 The movement of continents is known as continental drift. The German meteorologist, Alfred Wegener, first proposed the theory of continental drift in 1912. He said that continents were drifting across Earth's surface.

162 Alfred Wegener believed that millions of years ago there was a single continent named Pangaea, which broke apart over time. Its pieces drifted across the ocean to form the various continents. This also opened up water channels that became oceans.

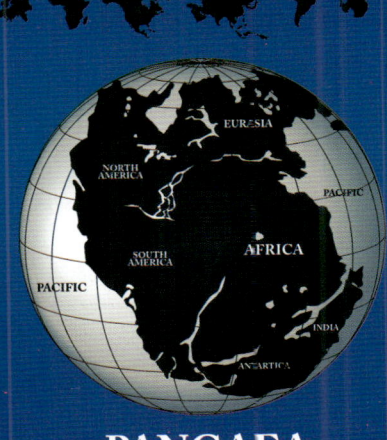

PANGAEA

PHYSICAL GEOGRAPHY

163

Even before Wegener, geologists had speculated that all existing continents came from a single landmass. Yet Wegener was the first to put forward a more believable theory with evidence he had collected over time.

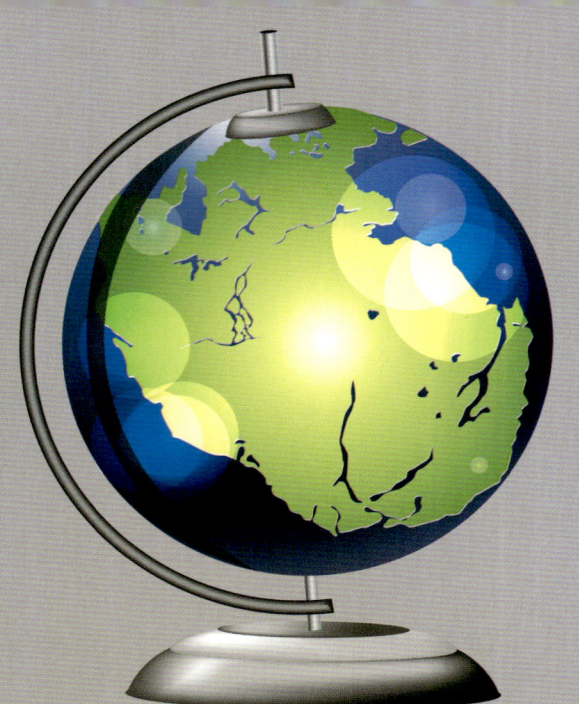

164

Wegener, who was also a biologist, used fossils to explain his theory. For instance, he found fossils of tropical plants in the frigid conditions of the Arctic region. He also found fossils of the same organisms in two separate continents, which suggested that the two continents had at one point been much closer.

MOVING CONTINENTS

165 You can actually see one of Wegener's evidences. Check the world map and you will notice that the South American east coast and the African west coast are perfectly aligned! Wegener thought that the two were joined together at some point and later drifted apart.

CONTINENTAL DRIFT

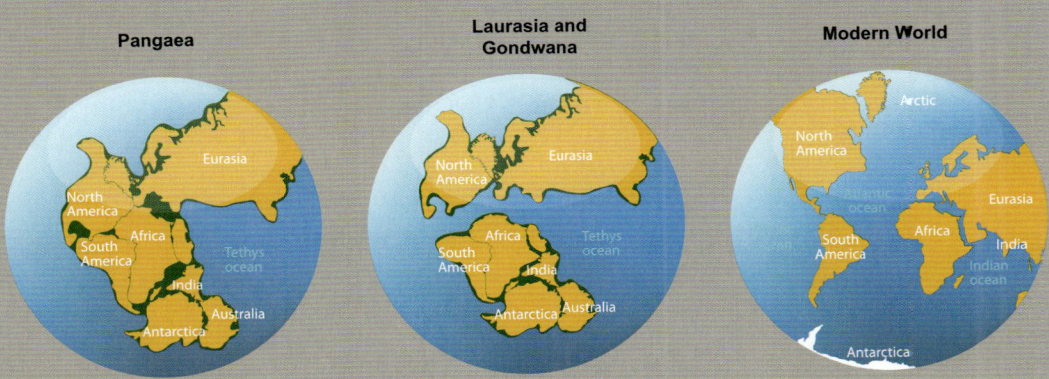

166 South African geologist, Alexander L. Du Toit, later came up with another modification. He suggested the existence of two primitive continents — Laurasia in the north and Gondwana in the south. Like Pangaea, these two also broke apart into smaller continents.

167 Today, scientists think that Pangaea, Laurasia and Gondwana were not the only three supercontinents to have existed. They believe that many such supercontinents have broken up and realigned over Earth's long history. Interestingly, Wegener's theory was actually rejected at the beginning.

PHYSICAL GEOGRAPHY

168 We now know that continents are always moving. Millions of years from today, the Earth will once again look completely different. For instance, Africa is slowly moving towards Europe and will one day merge with it.

169 The movement of Africa towards Europe is also changing Europe's geography. It is pushing up the Alps and the Pyrenees mountains and causing earthquakes in Turkey and Greece.

170 The movement of continents also affects oceans. For instance, the merging of Africa and Europe will close up the Mediterranean Sea, while widening the Atlantic Ocean. In fact, the Mediterranean Sea was probably much wider in the past.

MOVING CONTINENTS

171 **The reason for the widening of the Atlantic Ocean is the mid-Atlantic ridge.** It is an underwater ridge where molten magma is constantly spilling out, widening the ridge and the seafloor.

172 **The movement of continents will push America even farther away from Europe and Africa.** The Australian continent is also on the move, going north towards Asia. In fact, the process of this change is already going on.

173 **Today, scientists believe that other supercontinents have existed before Pangaea.** They break up and come together again and again. According to this theory, millions of years from today, all continents may merge into a single continent again, which is known as Pangaea Ultima.

174 **What drives this movement of continents?** What can move such massive landmasses? The answer lies in plate tectonics. Underneath the continents and oceans are tectonic plates that are constantly moving.

Movement of Tectonic Plates

175 Just like the layers in the atmosphere, Earth's crust has many layers as well. The outer layer is a hard, tough shell known as the lithosphere. The lithosphere is broken into large pieces known as tectonic plates. All the oceans and continents lie on these plates.

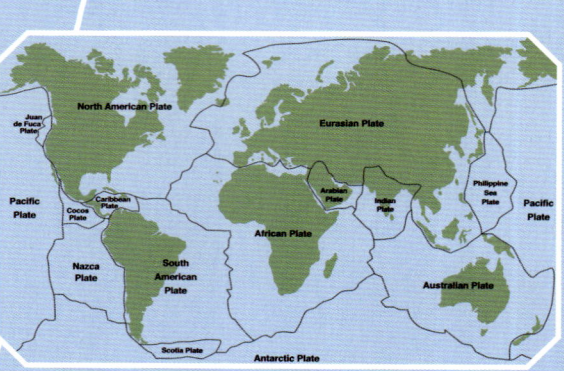

176 The plates are divided into a few major plates and a dozen or so minor plates. The major plates are named after the continents or oceans that are embedded upon them, such as the North American, Pacific and African plates.

MOVEMENT OF TECTONIC PLATES

177 **The tectonic plates are not static.** They are almost always moving. This movement in relation to other plates causes the many geographic and geological processes that shape the Earth's surface, such as volcanoes, earthquakes and the formation of surface features like mountains.

178 **Why do the tectonic plates move?** The answer lies in the Earth's molten core and mantle. The lithosphere rests on an underlying layer of molten rock, which is weaker and denser. The churning currents in this layer propel the plates to slide and move.

179 **The point where two plates interact is known as a plate boundary.** According to geologists, there are three types of boundaries: convergent, divergent and transform. It is at these boundaries that the Earth's surface constantly keeps changing.

PHYSICAL GEOGRAPHY

180 **At a convergent boundary, the plates move towards each other.** As a result, the two plates may crumble or one plate may dive under the other. Since it usually involves the destruction of plates, this boundary is also known as a destructive plate boundary.

Convergent plate boundary created by two continental plates that slide towards each other

181 **A convergent plate boundary is also where you will find many volcanoes and earthquakes.** As one plate dives under another, the overlying plate is pushed up, creating a mountain. The diving plate's molten temperature can sometimes result in the creation of volcanoes.

182 **Convergent plate boundaries under the ocean can cause deep trenches.** One such example is the Mariana Trench, the deepest point on Earth. It can also create volcanoes and mountains that can slowly pile up to form islands.

MOVEMENT OF TECTONIC PLATES

Divergent (Constructive) boundary occurs where two plates slide apart from each other.

183 **In divergent boundaries, the plates move away from each other.** At some boundaries, molten magma rises up, pushing the plates further away. It can also create giant trenches, such as the 6,000-km long Great Rift Valley in Africa.

184 **Can you name the longest mountain range in the world?** It is the mid-ocean ridge system, which lies under the ocean. It is also the best example of a divergent boundary where the magma has piled up to create the longest mountain chain.

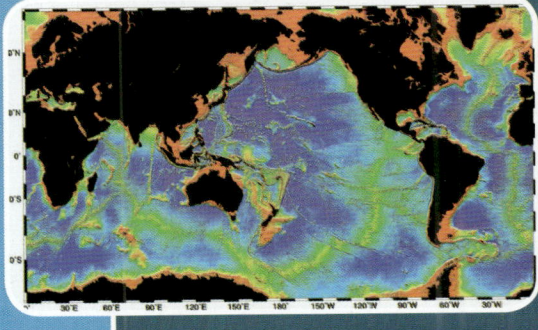

PHYSICAL GEOGRAPHY

185 At transform boundaries, the plates grind past each other. Sometimes this can create enough friction to cause an earthquake. An example of the transform boundary is the San Andreas Fault, which is the boundary between the Pacific and the North American plate.

186 Tectonic plates are responsible for Earth's unique geography. Over the years, they have created mountains, valleys, troughs and trenches. The highest and lowest points on Earth are often the result of movement of the tectonic plates.

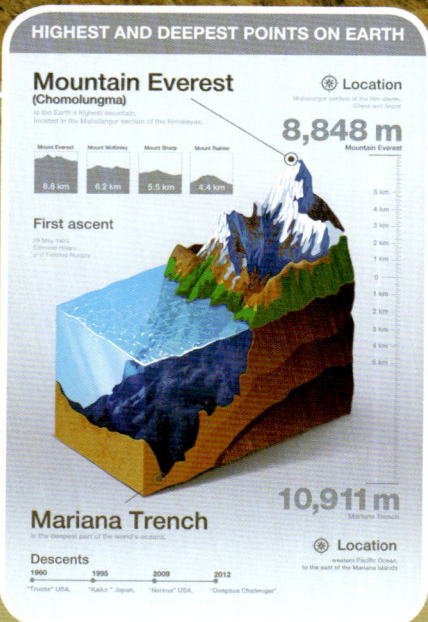

187 If tectonic plates are moving all the time, why do we not notice it? We do not notice the movement of tectonic plates because the speed of their movement is very slow, usually just a few centimetres in a year — sometimes slower than the growth of your nails!

MOVEMENT OF TECTONIC PLATES

188 **Sometimes, the plate movement is so drastic that it can cause havoc and destruction.** For instance, the magma that erupts at boundaries produces volcanoes, and jarring transform boundaries can cause devastating earthquakes.

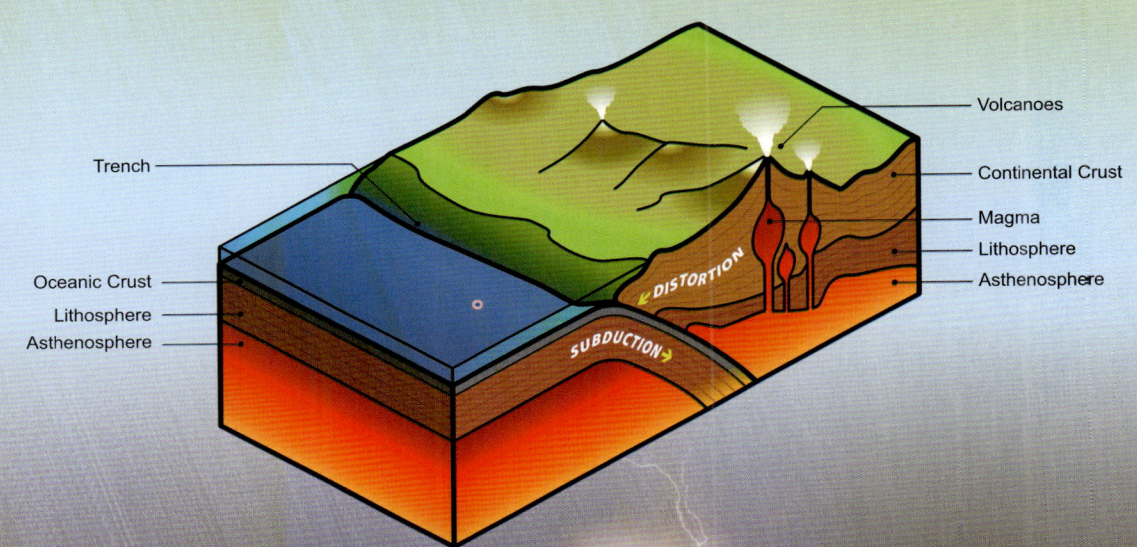

189 **Do you know there are volcanoes and earthquakes on the ocean floor?** When an earthquake occurs on the ocean floor, it causes a swell in the ocean waves. A small swell gains massive momentum as it rushes to the shore and becomes a tsunami.

Mountains

190 **Mountains are one of the most striking evidences of tectonic plate activity.** When two plates crash against each other, the crust folds and is pushed up. Slowly, the crust is pushed higher and higher, becoming a mountain.

191 **How are mountains different from hills?** To qualify as a mountain, an area must climb to a height of 1,000 feet above the surrounding land. Any elevation lower than that is usually known as a hill. A mountain range is a series of mountains linked together.

192 **Did you know that some mountains are still growing?** This is usually because the underlying plates are still pushing into each other. For instance, many mountains in the Himalayan range, including the highest mountain, Mt Everest, are still growing.

193 **Stretching over 2,900 km, the Himalayan range is the tallest mountain range in the world.** It has several peaks above 8,000 m, including Mount Everest, the highest peak in the world (8,48m). The next closest range in height is Aconcagua, in the Andes, which is 6,961m tall.

194 The Himalayan range was formed as a result of the Indo-Australian and Eurasian plates colliding against each other. Apart from creating these peaks, the collision has also resulted in a high number of earthquakes and tremors in the area.

195 The Himalayas, the tallest mountain range in the world, contains fossils of several coastal creatures. This is clear evidence that it was formed as a result of the coming together of two plates. The collision pushed up the coastline that contained the fossils.

196 Some mountains are formed because of volcanic eruptions. Molten magma from the Earth's interior erupts from cracks in the crust and piles up. Examples of volcanic mountains include Mount Fuji in Japan and St. Helens in the USA.

PHYSICAL GEOGRAPHY

197 **Sometimes, the magma will push up the crust, but harden before it can be ejected.** This results in the formation of dome mountains, such as the Adirondack Mountains of New York. Similarly, plateau mountains are formed when plates collide and push up the crust without deforming it.

198 **Do you know which is the tallest mountain in the world? Surprisingly, it is not very clear.** Everest is the tallest from sea level, but the farthest peak from the Earth's centre is Chimborazo. Also, if measured from its base, the tallest mountain is the half-submerged Mauna Kea mountain in Hawaii!

199 **Did you know that there are mountains deep under the ocean?** Formed due to underwater volcanic eruptions, these mountains sometimes rise above the ocean floor. These underwater mountains are known as seamounts.

MOUNTAINS

200 There are thousands of seamounts on the ocean floor, probably more than we have on land. Despite this, we know very little about them. Some seamounts, such as Mauna Kea, may grow out of the ocean surface.

201 Can you name the longest mountain range in the world? Above ground, it is the 7,000-km long Andes range of South America. But if we include seamounts, the longest range lies underwater — the mid-ocean ridge system that stretches over 65,000 kms.

202 The mid-ocean ridge was created when two ocean plates moved apart, resulting in the eruption of molten rocks and magma. This sediment built up over millions of years, creating this extensive range of mountains. It is actually a collection of smaller, underwater mountain ranges that stretch across most of the world's oceanic region.

PHYSICAL GEOGRAPHY

203 **As a result of the constant tectonic plate movement, the mid-ocean ridge is also a site for constant earthquakes and volcanoes.** As the plates move apart, a new ocean floor is created.

204 **Whether underwater or above ground surface, mountains form important ecosystems on Earth.** On the surface, mountains are home to vibrant forests. Due to their interaction with sea currents and rich formations, seamounts are home to many species, even corals.

Ice and Glaciers

205 Almost 10 per cent of Earth's surface is covered in glaciers, ice caps and ice sheets. Found in and around the polar regions, glaciers contain 75 per cent of the planet's store of fresh water.

206 A glacier is a slow-moving mass of ice. We find glaciers on mountains, valleys and alpines. Continental glaciers are large in scale, covering large landmasses. They are also known as ice caps or ice sheets.

207 Glaciers are considered to be remnants of the ice age — a time when ice covered a large expanse of the planet. Scientists believe that the Earth has gone through at least eight ice ages and the glaciers are remnants of the last one.

208 Glaciers are formed when snow accumulates in one place over a period of time. As new snow keeps falling, the older snow gets more and more compact and dense, slowly transforming into ice.

PHYSICAL GEOGRAPHY

209 **Why do glaciers occupy such a small portion on Earth?** This is because glaciers require special conditions to exist. First, enough snow must fall to begin the process. Second, it must stay cold enough for the snow to accumulate and remain frozen!

210 **You may think that glaciers are just flowing rivers of ice, but in fact, not all glaciers are the same.** Polar glaciers, found in the polar regions, stay consistently below zero degree temperature. Temperate glaciers are found on mountain peaks where the temperature does not remain constant.

211 **What makes glaciers unique is their ability to move, unlike any other ice mass on Earth.** Glaciers also have tremendous capacity to cause erosion, change their surroundings as they move. Due to their sheer mass, they move quite slowly.

ICE AND GLACIERS

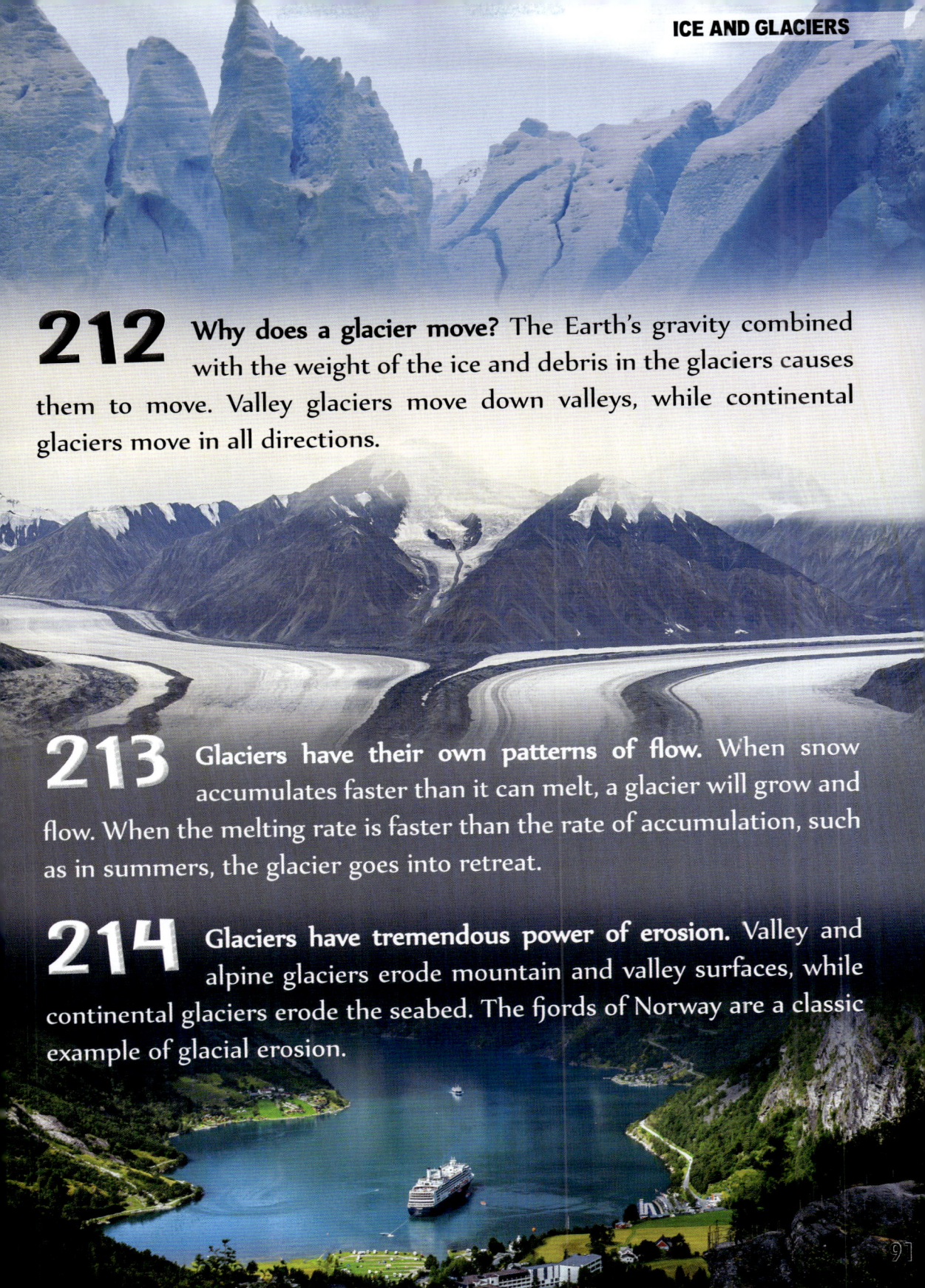

212 Why does a glacier move? The Earth's gravity combined with the weight of the ice and debris in the glaciers causes them to move. Valley glaciers move down valleys, while continental glaciers move in all directions.

213 Glaciers have their own patterns of flow. When snow accumulates faster than it can melt, a glacier will grow and flow. When the melting rate is faster than the rate of accumulation, such as in summers, the glacier goes into retreat.

214 Glaciers have tremendous power of erosion. Valley and alpine glaciers erode mountain and valley surfaces, while continental glaciers erode the seabed. The fjords of Norway are a classic example of glacial erosion.

PHYSICAL GEOGRAPHY

215 **Glacial retreat also affects the texture of the surrounding land.** Glaciers often carry sediments and as they retreat, they leave behind many of these, including rocks. Their edges can carve a valley, leaving behind pronounced jagged surfaces.

216 **The large expanse of continental glaciers (extending over 50,000 sq km), found in Greenland and Antarctica is known as an ice sheet.** When chunks of ice flow out from these sheets into the cold water, we get ice shelves.

217 **When chunks of ice break away from ice shelves or glaciers, we get icebergs.** The term 'iceberg' is used for chunks that are at least 5 metres wide. Smaller chunks are known as 'bergy bits' and 'growlers'.

ICE AND GLACIERS

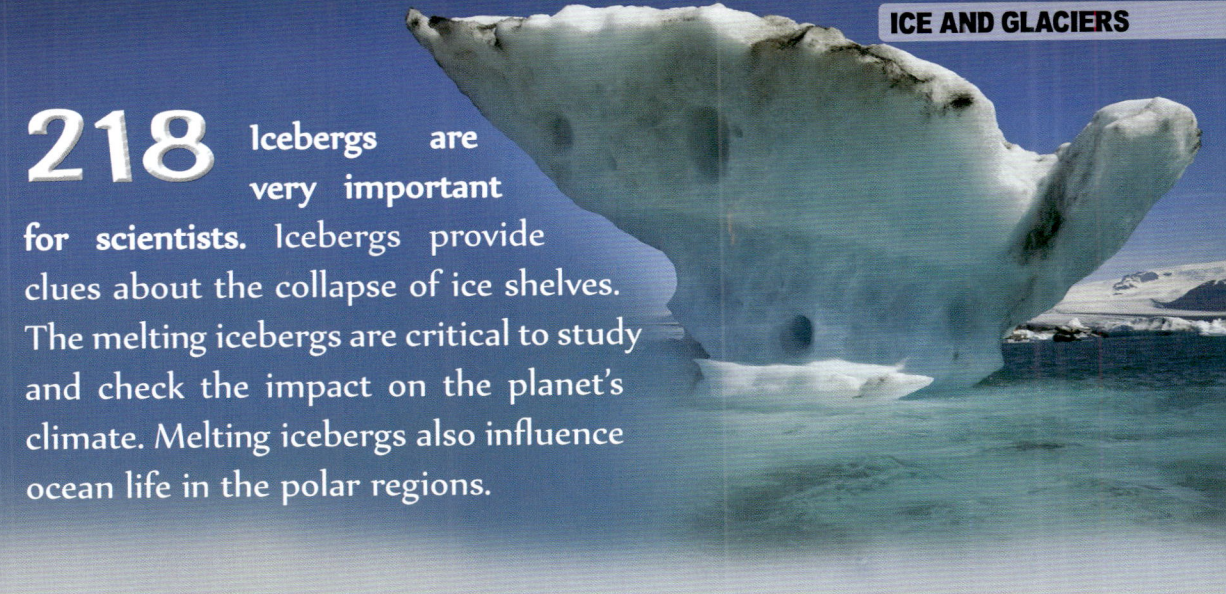

218 **Icebergs are very important for scientists.** Icebergs provide clues about the collapse of ice shelves. The melting icebergs are critical to study and check the impact on the planet's climate. Melting icebergs also influence ocean life in the polar regions.

219 **What will happen if all the glaciers melted today?** Scientists estimate that a global glacial melt will raise sea levels by 230 feet, submerging all coastal areas. Alarmingly, at the rate at which global warming is taking place means that such a day may happen pretty soon.

Polar and Tundra Regions

220 Tundra regions are the Earth's coldest and harshest biospheres. They are found in the Arctic and on mountain tops which have low temperatures and are mostly covered with ice. Such regions are found in both the northern and southern hemispheres.

221 The polar regions are the areas around the two poles of Earth, which fall in the Frigid Zones. The two poles are found in the continent of Antarctica and on the Arctic Ocean. They are covered in ice, which is known as the polar ice caps.

222 While polar regions are devoid of trees and other such vegetation, the tundra region is mainly covered in ice until the summer season brings in a bloom of flowers. Thus, it is cold, but also supports some vegetation.

223 The animals which survive in polar and tundra areas are specially adapted to live in such harsh conditions. Tundra regions have animals like mountain goats and birds as the dominant species, while in the polar regions, polar bears and arctic foxes are commonly found animals.

POLAR AND TUNDRA REGIONS

224 The animals which are accustomed to climate and conditions of specific areas are facing a grave future due to the threat of global warming. They are in the danger of losing their homes and becoming extinct!

225 Did you know that the arctic fox can only thrive in colder regions? In recent years, due to the increasing temperature of the polar regions, the southern fox species, such as the red fox, have also started living in the areas previously dominated by the arctic foxes, making food scarce and survival difficult.

226 Did you know that the penguins can sometimes accidentally ingest seaweed while hunting? They have a special gland in their body that helps them get rid of the salty water by sneezing.

PHYSICAL GEOGRAPHY

227 In the Arctic region, there is a layer of permafrost, which means a layer of permanently frozen ground. This does not let huge plants like trees take root in the ground. This is one of the reasons why one can hardly find any substantial vegetation in these areas.

228 Permafrost is a layer comprising plants and soil which freeze and are found under the surface of the soil. The layer found in the Arctic is believed to contain almost 14% of the world's carbon dioxide. Global warming is now causing this layer to melt, increasing risks of releasing the trapped gas into the environment.

229 Did you know that there are no polar bears in the antarctic tundra region of the southern hemisphere? They are only found in the northern hemisphere. An interesting fact is that only the fur of a polar bear is white. Its skin is dark, just like other bears.

POLAR AND TUNDRA REGIONS

230
Did you know that animals like the reindeers migrate from the tundra region during the winters in search of food and return when the climate becomes warmer? This seasonal migration is also seen among birds.

231
Did you know that the arctic foxes have not one but two coats? The first coat remains hidden under the thick white coat which grows during the winters and protects them from the cold.

232
The climate in the alpine regions does not allow for the growth of trees. This is because its harsh climate and high altitude make it difficult for trees to find the right growth conditions.

PHYSICAL GEOGRAPHY

233 Do you know where the lowest temperature ever was recorded? The lowest temperature (−89.2 °C) recorded at the surface was at Vostok Station in Antarctica. However, more recently, NASA satellites have recorded temperatures of −93.2 °C, also at Antarctica.

234 Have you heard of the Bearberry? It is a kind of dwarf shrub that is uniquely adapted to arctic conditions. It thrives in the tundra region and has many benefits when used in medicines.

Grasslands

235 Grasslands are famous for harbouring various species of grasses amongst other plants, as their dominant vegetation. They can be found in every continent, other than Antarctica.

236 Did you know that grasslands are ideal for growing crops? The reason for this is that grasslands usually have very fertile soil. At the same time, they are also widely used for pastureland.

237 A strange fact related to grasslands is that often people set fire to vast areas of grass. This is usually done to ensure that unwanted plants do not breed excessively and destroy the natural vegetation.

PHYSICAL GEOGRAPHY

238 **The tropical grasslands and the temperate grasslands are differentiated because of the weather conditions of the areas they thrive in.** While tropical grasslands experience warm weather for most part of the year, the temperate grasslands experience both warm weather conditions and cold weather conditions at different times of the year.

239 **Some of the grasslands in the United States have seen such destruction due to farming that the government has converted some farming areas into grasslands by growing grasses on them.**

GRASSLANDS

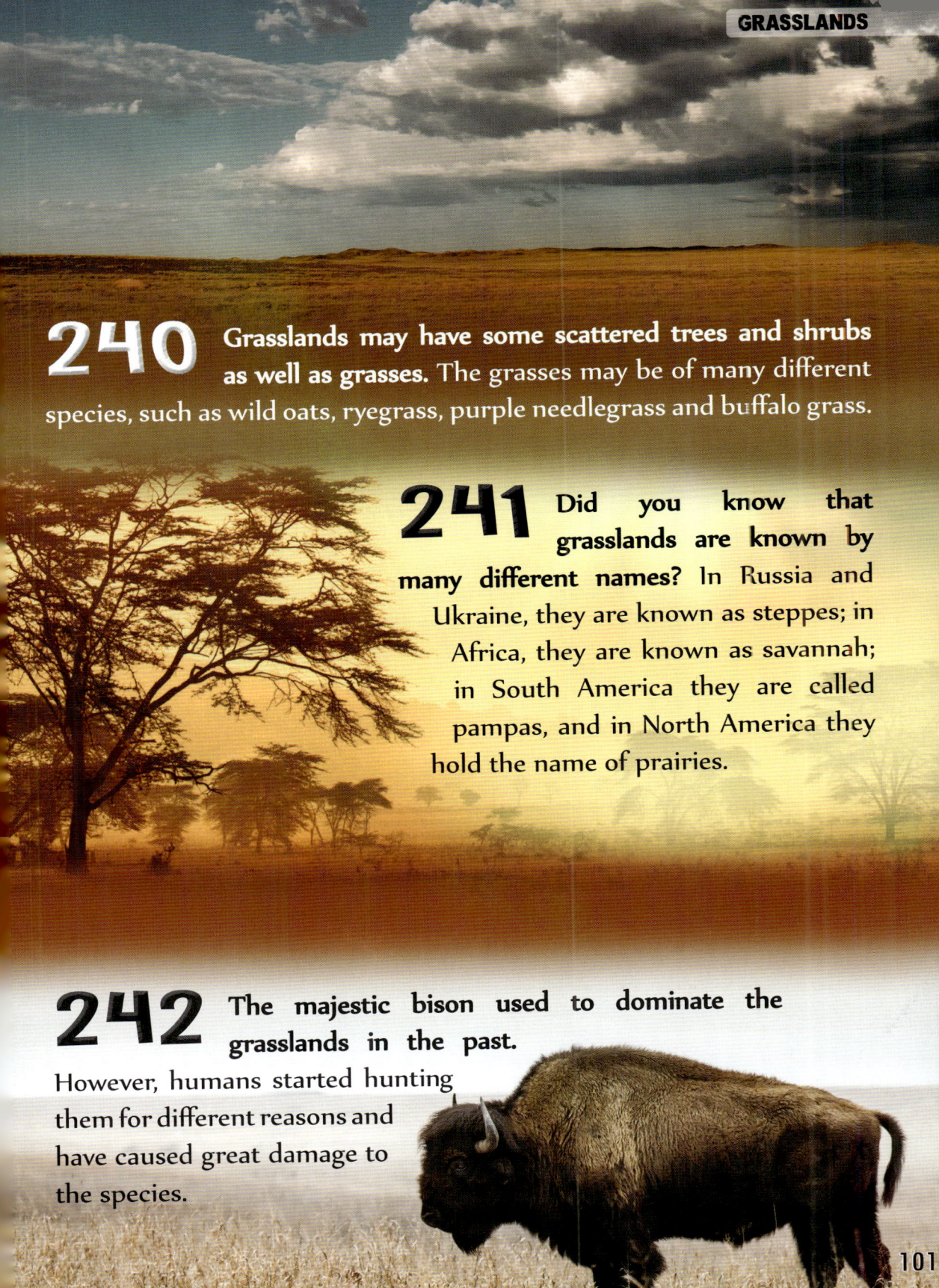

240 Grasslands may have some scattered trees and shrubs as well as grasses. The grasses may be of many different species, such as wild oats, ryegrass, purple needlegrass and buffalo grass.

241 Did you know that grasslands are known by many different names? In Russia and Ukraine, they are known as steppes; in Africa, they are known as savannah; in South America they are called pampas, and in North America they hold the name of prairies.

242 The majestic bison used to dominate the grasslands in the past. However, humans started hunting them for different reasons and have caused great damage to the species.

PHYSICAL GEOGRAPHY

243 Did you know that only about 2% of the original spread of grasslands remains in North America today? All the rest have been cleared for farming and human activity!

244 Even though the grasslands seem to be have sparse vegetation over the ground, beneath the soil they see deep and extensive root systems. This ensures that the grasses can flourish even in windy and harsh weather conditions.

245 Temperate grasslands are less likely to support shrubs and trees than tropical grasslands. This is because of the weather conditions as well as poor soil quality.

246 Did you know that the grasses grow fast because their points which promote growth are located close to the ground? Therefore, no matter how much the animals graze on them, the grass cover is able to recover quite fast.

247 Due to overgrazing and soil erosion, the natural grasslands are facing the danger of getting destroyed. They support unique species of animals which in turn are facing the threat of extinction.

248 Did you know that grasslands mainly occur between the desert and forest areas? It is interesting to note that most grassland soils have nutrients that can only be accessed for plants by ploughing. That is why grasslands don't support many plants naturally, but make for excellent farming land.

249 There are three kinds of savannahs. Those formed due to natural climatic conditions are called climatic savannahs. The ones formed because of human activities are called derived savannahs. The ones caused by soil habits are called edaphic savannahs.

Wetlands

250 **Wetlands are one of the most unique ecosystems found on Earth.** To be called a wetland, the area must be soaked with water for some part of the year. That's right! Some wetlands are actually dry at certain times of the year.

251 **Wetlands act as the transition zone between land and water.** They are usually present along the boundaries of streams, lakes, ponds, or even in large shallow holes that fill up with rainwater. Some common names for different types of wetlands are swamp, marsh, and bog.

WETLANDS

252 When water flows through the wetlands, it slows down due to dense vegetation. The slowing water causes sediments and pollutants to settle on the bottom. Here the water soaks into the ground to help fill aquifers and other sources of groundwater.

253 An acre of wetland can store one–1.5 million gallons of floodwater! When it rains, the wetlands fill with water and slowly release water over time. By filtering, cleaning, and storing water, wetlands act like kidneys for other ecosystems!

254 Freshwater wetlands have a variety of plants, and each different type of wetland may have different kinds of plants. For example, cypress trees grow in freshwater swamps, and have knobs or 'knees' that grow above the roots. These knees emerge from the water and help in absorbing oxygen.

PHYSICAL GEOGRAPHY

255 Some wetland trees grow prop roots that make them appear to be standing on stilts above the water. These trees are found in mangrove forests. These forests get flooded by tides at least twice every day. This tangle of roots prevents the trees from drowning in water. They also help in slowing down the flow of the tides. There are about 80 different species of mangrove trees!

256 Some plants found in wetlands appear to be floating! The duckweed plant extends its roots down into the water to absorb nutrients. It is not attached to the bottom and floats freely. Cattails and sedges also grow up from the soil, through the water.

257 Standing waters of the wetlands form the perfect environment for amphibians to lay their eggs and wait for the tadpoles to grow. No wonder amphibians, like frogs and salamanders, abound in the wetlands! So the next time you visit a wetland, look forward to hearing the calls of frogs!

WETLANDS

258 Wetlands are home to a great variety of birds. Many birds rely on wetland habitat for breeding and raising their young ones. Many migratory birds come down to rest in the wetlands while flying along migratory routes. Wetlands form the nestling or feeding spots for up to half of North American bird species.

259 Mosquitoes thrive in areas that have standing water. And the damp condition of the wetlands is perfect for that! Make sure to carry your mosquito repellent when you visit a wetland. On the bright side, insects like mosquitoes help in pollinating plants and providing food for birds and amphibians.

PHYSICAL GEOGRAPHY

260 Not a long time ago, many people thought of wetlands as dark, damp and scary places. People believed that wetlands were full of snakes, alligators and mosquitoes. It is for this reason that a big wetland in southern Virginia was named 'The Great Dismal Swamp'.

261 Wetlands were once considered useless and dangerous. So people thought that it was best to drain wetlands and make way for cities and farms. It is estimated that half of the world's wetlands have been destroyed since 1900.

262 Destruction of wetland is leading to a loss of habitat for many species found only in the wetlands. The Florida manatee is one such endangered bird that is at a risk of becoming extinct because of the destruction of wetlands for residential developments.

WETLANDS

263 **Rise in temperature is causing ice in the Polar regions to melt and sea levels to increase.** As a result, the shallow wetlands are being flooded and some species of mangrove trees are being drowned. On the other hand, wetlands such as estuaries, floodplains and marshes are getting destroyed through drought.

264 **With their rich biodiversity, wetlands can be a treat for nature lovers!** The presence of waterfowl, songbirds, raptors, and shorebirds attracts hoards of birdwatchers. Wetlands also make perfect spots for recreational activities such as hunting, fishing, canoeing and wildlife photography.

Deserts

265 Dry, barren and desolate are the words we associate with deserts. Generally speaking, a desert is an area that tends to lose more moisture through evaporation than it receives from annual precipitation. Deserts receive less than 25 centimetres of annual rainfall.

266 It is true that a great part of Earth is covered in water. But did you know, almost one-third of Earth's land surface is desert, and that share is growing every year! Deserts are found on every continent.

267 Believe it or not, there are parts of the Atacama Desert in Chile where no rainfall has ever been recorded! And yet it is home to more than one million people. Farmers extract enough water from underground aquifers and streams to grow crops and raise llamas and alpacas.

DESERTS

268 They say desperate times call for desperate measures! Well, it seems to be true in the case of the scarab beetle found in the Sahara Desert. It is also known as the 'dung beetle' because it can survive almost entirely on animal faeces. The beetles roll a ball of dung to lay eggs in and build their burrows next to a heap of it.

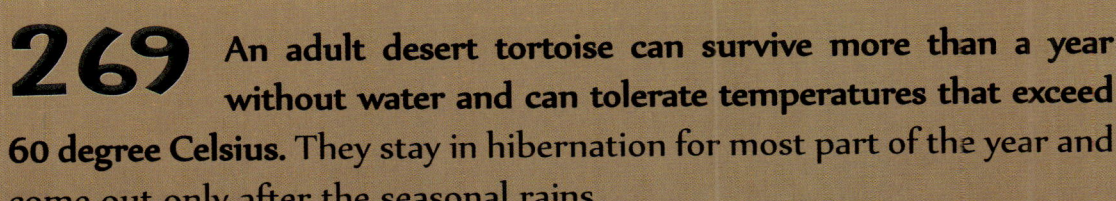

269 An adult desert tortoise can survive more than a year without water and can tolerate temperatures that exceed 60 degree Celsius. They stay in hibernation for most part of the year and come out only after the seasonal rains.

PHYSICAL GEOGRAPHY

270 **Daytime in the desert can be very hard to bear.** No wonder many animals that live in the desert are nocturnal! They hide out in their burrows during the day and come out at night to hunt for food and to mate when it's cooler. Coyotes, skunks, bobcats, tarantulas, scorpions, centipedes, kangaroo rats, jack rabbits, owls and nightjars are some desert animals that you might spot at night.

271 **Turns out that most of the desert plants have excellent survival skills!** They have adapted to the arid climate by growing long roots that tap water from deep underground. Many desert plants can even live for a hundred years.

272 **Cacti have special means of storing and conserving water.** If you get lost in the desert, you can try your luck by picking a prickly pear cactus for water and nourishment. But be careful, some species of cacti could give you headaches and diarrhoea!

DESERTS

273 Who says a desert must always be scorching hot? The largest desert in the world is Antarctica. With an average annual precipitation of only eight inches, Antarctica is quite dry! Another cold desert is the Gobi Desert in Asia.

274 The Sahara in North Africa is the largest hot desert in the world. Despite being a desert, Sahara has been home to people for centuries. That is because of the River Nile that flows through the desert. Some of the sand dunes found there are as high as a whopping 500 feet!

275 The Gobi desert in Mongolia is one of the harshest deserts in the world. But once upon a time, it was home to a marvellous variety of plants and animals. The first dinosaur eggs were found among the fossils in the red rocks of this cold and desolate desert.

PHYSICAL GEOGRAPHY

276 According to the calculations of German physicist Gerhard Knies, the world's deserts receive more energy from the sun in merely six hours than what humans consume in a year. That means, an 8,100-square-mile stretch of Sahara desert could power a continent about the size of Europe!

277 Did you know that deserts don't always form naturally? Sometimes they form because of loss of plant cover due to misuse of land. When cattle graze in the same spots for a long time, the plant cover starts disappearing. Fire could also be one of the reasons for loss of vegetation as it can destroy everything in its path.

278 Loss of plant cover on a large scale is forming deserts all over the world. This process is called desertification. About 46,000 square miles of land turns to desert every year due to climate change and deforestation. According to the UN, livelihoods of more than one billion people in 110 countries are threatened by desertification.

DESERTS

279 **Desertification across the world has been causing deadly dust storms.** The Chinese are trying to deal with it by planting a Green Great Wall of shrubs and trees. It will stretch 2,800 miles from outer Beijing through Inner Mongolia. It is hoped that some parts of the Gobi Desert may start showing signs of vegetation, thanks to these new plantations.

280 **Some villagers in Burkina Faso, Africa, came up with a rather creative plan to prevent desertification.** The village increased crop yields by 50% simply by arranging stones in order to prevent the rainwater from getting washed away, and digging pits to collect the water.

281 **For those who love deserts and adventure, an annual ultramarathon is held each year in the Sahara Desert.** It's called the Marathon des Sables. It is a six-day, 156 mile trek through the sands. It goes without saying that it is considered to be the hardest foot race on the planet.

Forests

282 Białowieża Forest in Poland and Belarus is the largest and one of the last primeval forests, which once covered the European countries. The ground is a bio reserve and is protected by numerous laws.

283 Did you know that a compound called pinene which is found in pine trees acts as an anti-inflammatory substance and makes the lungs feel fresher?

284 A tree named pando in Utah is so huge that it has spread its roots in a large region which in turn have sprouted trunks, hence creating a whole forest in the process! This tree is a quaking aspen tree.

FORESTS

285 There is a primeval underwater forest off the Alabama Coast in the Gulf of Mexico which is believed to be 50,000 years old! It is a Bald Cypress forest which was discovered in the year 2005 after Hurricane Katrina uncovered it.

286 Humans have destroyed forests since a very long time and continue to do so even today. Till date, we have collectively destroyed almost 80% of the natural forests on Earth!

287 Have you ever wondered which is the largest living organism on the planet? Well, it is a huge mushroom known as honey mushroom in Oregon! It has been measured to be approximately 3.8 km wide.

117

PHYSICAL GEOGRAPHY

288 The Three-North Shelter Forest Program is a program in China where artificial forest land is being created to stop further expansion of desert land. Other similar projects are being considered around the world.

289 Did you know that it is believed that more than 90% of the old-growth redwood forest in California has been stripped off? This could have very serious ecological repercussions.

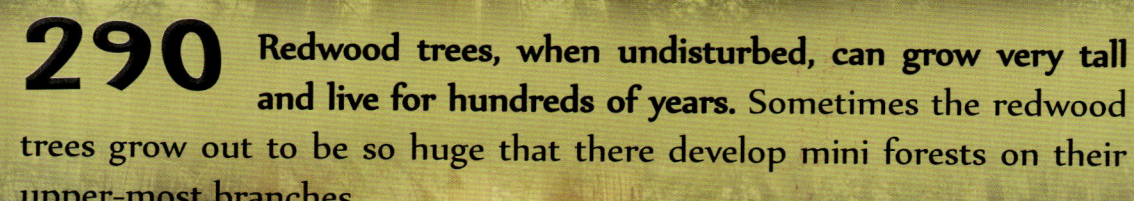

290 Redwood trees, when undisturbed, can grow very tall and live for hundreds of years. Sometimes the redwood trees grow out to be so huge that there develop mini forests on their upper-most branches.

FORESTS

291 Did you know that the International Forests Day was coined by the United Nations on 21 March, 2012? It was created to increase awareness about the importance of forest conservation.

292 It is believed that the forests are re-establishing themselves in some of the countries, such as North America and Europe. However, it is our responsibility to do our bit for reforestation as well.

293 Did you know that a satellite-run programme called the Global Forest Watch lets people map deforestation in real time? It is a very disturbing fact that despite government efforts and global awareness, people still don't recognise the harmful effects of cutting trees in large numbers.

PHYSICAL GEOGRAPHY

294 A report by the United Nations states that almost 13% of the world's forests today are conserved as biodiversity areas. They are very important for the health of the Earth.

295 The world's largest forest cover is believed to be the taiga region, which covers areas in Alaska and Canada amongst other countries.

296 Did you know that tropical rainforests are so thick that at times it takes a few minutes for the rain drops to reach the ground, while it makes its way through the dense canopy?

ROCKS

Rocks and Minerals

297 You may be amazed to know that according to scientists, there are around 5,000 known minerals on Earth. Minerals are formed by geological processes and are naturally occurring substances. Scientists are always in the process of discovering new things, so there is a strong possibility of them finding many more kinds of minerals.

298 While some minerals are made of just one chemical, some are compounds of two or more chemicals. It is believed that minerals are generally made of 92 elements that join together in many different combinations. For instance, diamond comprises just carbon, while granite comprises quartz, feldspar and mica.

ROCKS

299 Quartz, a very common mineral found on Earth, is also one of the hardest crystals. Since quartz vibrates at a very specific frequency, it is used in watches to ensure correct reading of time.

300 A mineral's hardness is determined by the ease or difficulty with which it can be scratched by another mineral. This is measured on the Mohs scale of mineral hardness. Diamond is very hard and is rated at 10 on the Mohs scale whereas talc is very soft and is rated at 1.

301 Like vitamins, minerals also help our bodies to grow and stay healthy. They aid in the performance of different kind of functions, such as building strong bones and transmitting nerve impulses. Some minerals also help in the production of certain hormones and in maintaining normal heartbeat.

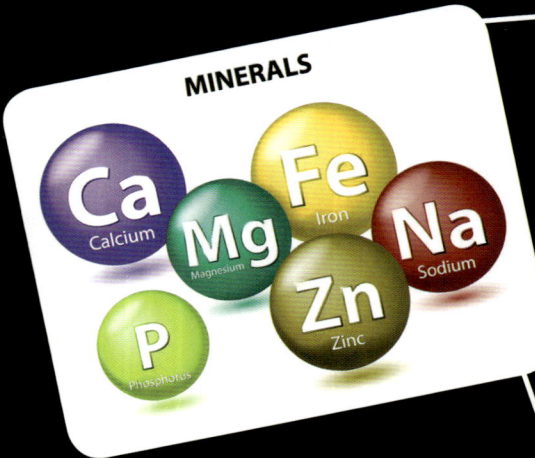

ROCKS AND MINERALS

302 You may find it interesting to know that calcium helps us to do many things, such as build strong and healthy teeth to chew our food with and strengthen bones that help us stand up straight. Calcium also makes us strong so we can play sports.

303 Minerals are generally divided into two groups: silicates and non-silicates. Minerals that contain silicon and oxygen are known as silicates, while others are categorised as non-silicates. You may be amazed to know that more than 90 per cent of the Earth's crust is made up of silicates.

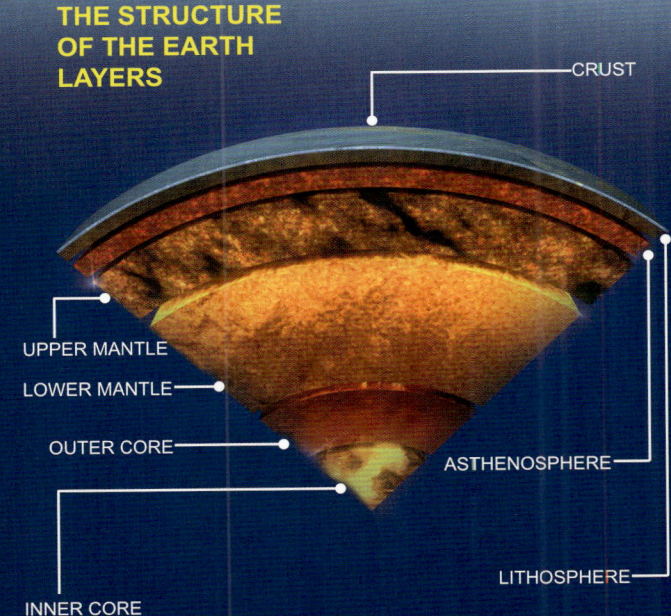

THE STRUCTURE OF THE EARTH LAYERS
- CRUST
- UPPER MANTLE
- LOWER MANTLE
- OUTER CORE
- INNER CORE
- ASTHENOSPHERE
- LITHOSPHERE

304 Do you know why you feel thirsty after eating salty food, like pizza? This is because the sodium level in your blood plasma becomes concentrated, and in order to dilute this, the blood pulls water out of your body cells. This sends a distress signal of dehydration to your brain, which in turn sends a signal to you to drink water.

ROCKS

305 Some minerals are colourful. Early humans often ground up minerals and used them to make paints. Some examples of colourful minerals are copper, cinnabar and blue lapis lazuli.

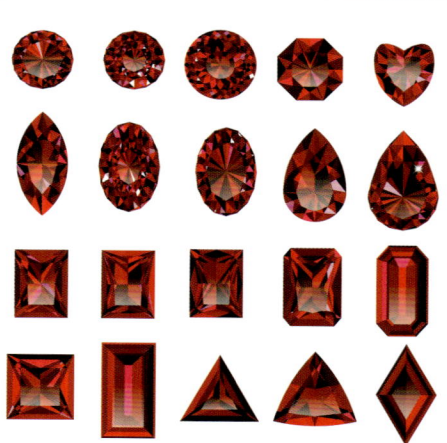

306 Have you seen beautiful ruby gems? These gems are in fact the mineral corundum in its red form. Corundum is generally made of trace mixtures of iron, titanium and chromium. The red colour of a ruby is due to the traces of chromium in corundum. Nowadays, rubies are also created synthetically in labs.

307 Do you know why we consume iodized salt? Iodine is an important mineral for our growth and its deficiency can lead to a health issue known as goitre. Since the Earth's soil is low in iodine content, this important mineral continues to be added to our table salt since the 1920s to meet the consumption needs of human beings.

308 **You may have seen marble floors in many houses and hotels.** These white and black coloured slabs are nothing but a type of metamorphic rock composed of carbonate minerals. Marble is water resistant. It is generally used to make sculptures and as a building material.

309 It is interesting to know that one of the first minerals to ever be recorded was jade, found in Mesopotamia, around 5000 B.C. People used it to create beads because of its colour (shades of green and turquoise). In ancient times, people used jade to make sharp and strong items like hammers, knives, fishhooks and axes.

310 **Do you know what feldspar is?** It is the term used for a very large group of minerals found in abundance on Earth. It is also very interesting to know that half of the Earth's crust is made up of feldspar: approximately 60% of the continental crust or 49% of the lithosphere.

311 Olivine is a special group of rock-forming minerals. It is a very common mineral found on our planet, nearly 80 per cent by volume. The gemstone peridot is a variety of this mineral. Olivine is also the major component in volcanic lava.

312 Soapstone has been so named because it feels like soap to the touch. This is because this stone is mainly composed of talc, which is the softest mineral. Soapstone has the ability to absorb heat, as well as radiate heat, due to which it is used to make cooking pots, bowls, cooking slabs, knife blades and spearheads.

ROCKS AND MINERALS

313 Did you know that some rocks glow in the dark? Some minerals have impurities known as activators due to which they fluoresce under UV light. When these activators get stuck in their high-energy state, the mineral continues to glow after the UV light is turned off. This phenomenon is known as phosphorescence.

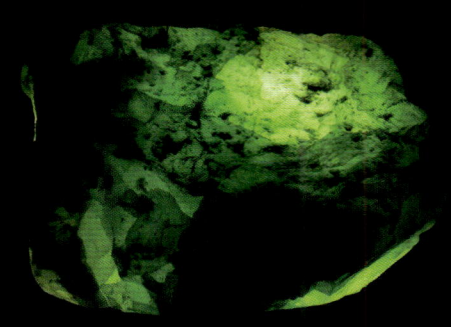

314 You may be amazed to know that the different colours in fireworks come from the presence of different minerals. The gold sparks in fireworks are produced by iron fillings and charcoal; bright flashes and loud bangs come from aluminium powder; and strontium, copper and halite produce red, blue and yellow sparks, respectively.

315 The water from the famous Epsom spring was popularised in England during the 1600s. It became known as a curative, used as an internal remedy and blood purifier. It is really interesting to know that in the year 1695, Doctor Nehemiah Grew isolated salt in the form of magnesium sulphate from the Epsom spring waters. This was the birth of the famous Epsom Salt.

ROCKS

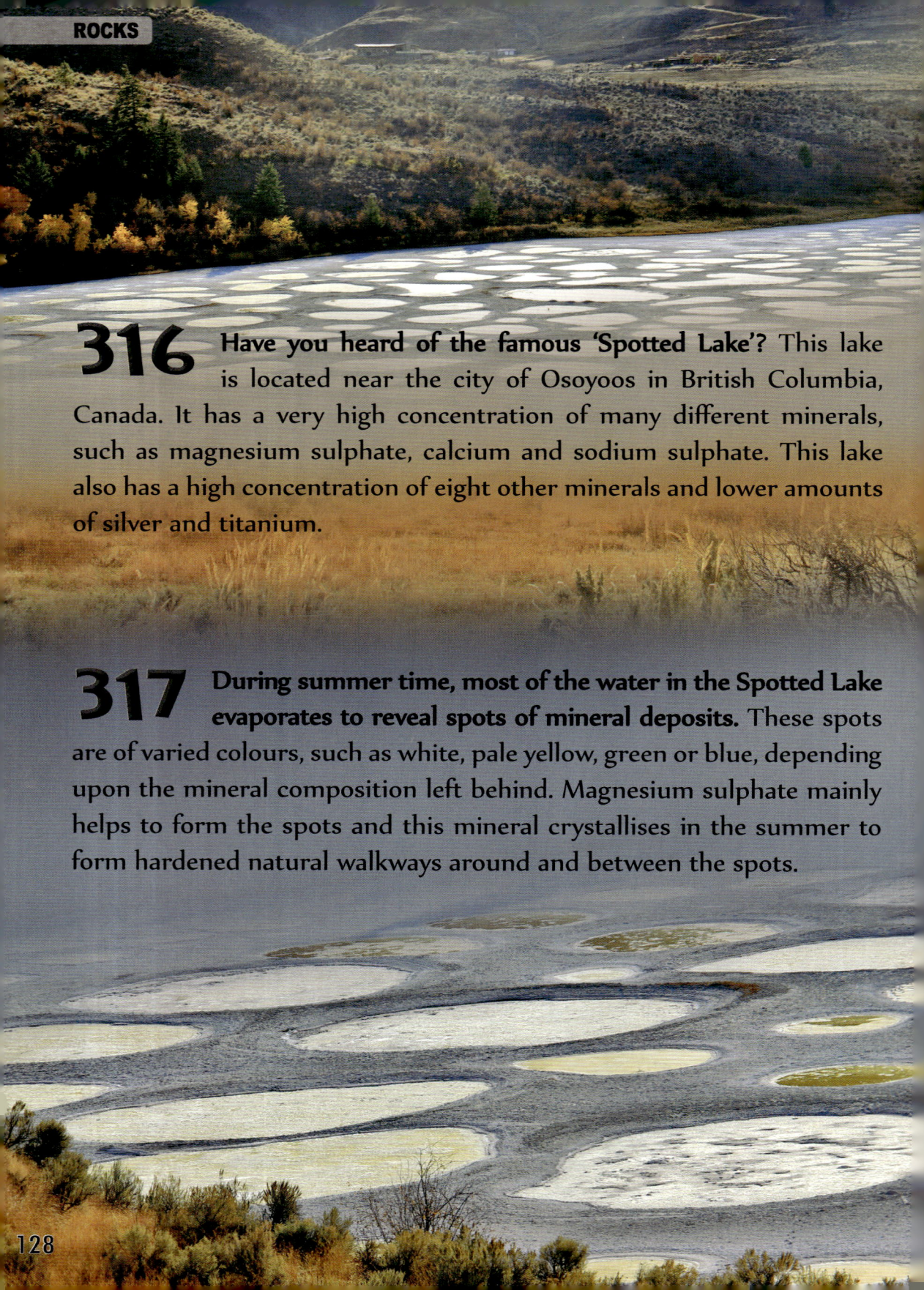

316 Have you heard of the famous 'Spotted Lake'? This lake is located near the city of Osoyoos in British Columbia, Canada. It has a very high concentration of many different minerals, such as magnesium sulphate, calcium and sodium sulphate. This lake also has a high concentration of eight other minerals and lower amounts of silver and titanium.

317 During summer time, most of the water in the Spotted Lake evaporates to reveal spots of mineral deposits. These spots are of varied colours, such as white, pale yellow, green or blue, depending upon the mineral composition left behind. Magnesium sulphate mainly helps to form the spots and this mineral crystallises in the summer to form hardened natural walkways around and between the spots.

ROCKS AND MINERALS

318 **Another amazing fact about the Spotted Lake is that minerals from this lake were harvested for manufacturing ammunition during the First World War.** It is believed that Chinese labourers would ship salts in quantities of about a tonne a day from the surface of this lake to munitions factories in Eastern Canada.

319 **We generally think that rocks are hard and solid, but you may be amazed to know that even sand and mud are types of rocks.** It is hard for us to imagine, but rocks are used to build washing machines, video games, airplanes and cars as well.

320 **Have you heard of fulgurite rocks?** The story of the formation of these glassy rocks is very interesting. When lightning strikes beach sand, the heat of the light melts the sand to form a glassy rock known as 'fulgurite'. Some fulgurites take the form of tubes and can even exceed a diameter of about half an inch or more. The best-known fulgurites are found in quartz sand.

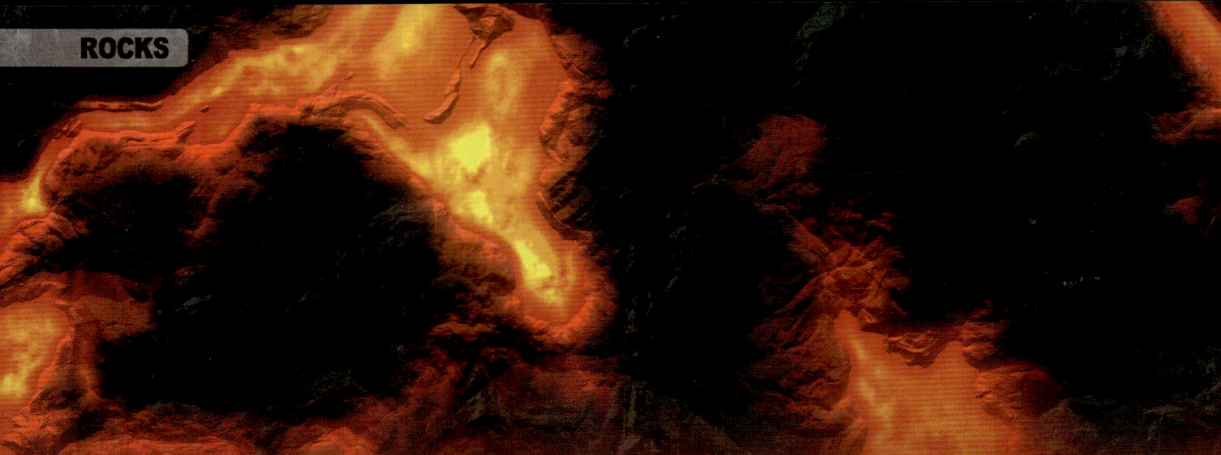

321 Magma is a hot molten rock that is made up of a mixture of liquid rock minerals and dissolved gases. It is found deep beneath the Earth's surface where the temperature is about 800 to 1200 degree Celsius — the temperature at which rocks can melt. Magma is called lava when it runs out onto the Earth's surface.

322 You may have heard of the word 'meteorites'. Do you know what they are? Simply put, meteorites are metals or rocks from space. These meteorites are solid piece of debris from objects like comets or asteroids that originate in outer space but survive the passage through the Earth's atmosphere.

323 Basalt is the most common rock found on Earth. This type of rock is formed when lava cools quickly. Interestingly, most of the ocean floor and the Hawaiian Islands are made up of basalt rocks. It is a commonly found type of rock and has been found on the surface of the Moon, as well as on Venus and Mars.

ROCKS AND MINERALS

324 Rocks have helped mankind since ancient times. Rocks led to the discovery of fire. Early humans used to rub together special kinds of rocks (flint) to produce fire. Rocks were also used for hunting, shelter and defence purposes.

325 Have you wondered where the sand on beaches comes from? When a rock breaks down, the material produced is known as sand. This breakdown of rock into sand happens over a long period of time —hundreds, thousands or millions of years.

326 Can you believe that there occurs in nature a rock from which you can extract oil? A rock known as oil shale contains significant amounts of kerogen, which can produce liquid oil if heated in the absence of oxygen. The oil thus produced is a substitute of crude oil. However, this is a really expensive way of extracting oil.

ROCKS

327 Scientists believe that Acasta Gneisses in Northwest Territories, Canada, near the Great Slave Lake, are among the oldest rocks found on Earth so far. The isua supracrustal belt in West Greenland is also considered to house some of the oldest rocks found on Earth.

328 A rock that contains adequate quantities of minerals along with vital elements, including metals, is known as an ore. These minerals and vital elements can be extracted from the rock using inexpensive methods. The ore is first extracted from the ground through mining and then it is refined to extract valuable elements.

Formation of Rocks

329 Do you know that in the structure of Earth, the lithosphere is a solid layer made up of rocks? It is also known as the Earth's outer surface. You can say that rocks are naturally occurring solid aggregates of minerals. A rock cycle is a geological process in which rocks are formed, worn down and then formed again.

330 The process of fractional crystallization plays an important part in the formation of igneous rocks. It is one of the many geochemical and physical processes that occur within the Earth's crust and mantle. Igneous rocks are formed from cooled magma, which is composed of various pre-existing rocks.

331 Evaporation or precipitation in a saturated mineral solution can lead to the formation of sedimentary rocks. Generally, sedimentary rocks are formed through the process of lithification — in which the deposition, accumulation and eventual cementation of sediments occurs in an organic manner.

332 It is interesting to know that metamorphic rocks are nothing but modified and denser forms of igneous and sedimentary rocks. They are formed due to physical and chemical alterations caused by heat and pressure of existing igneous or sedimentary rocks. This can happen because of various factors, such as the action of tectonic plates, compression, stress, etc. over a long period of time.

Igneous Rocks

333 Andesite is a form of igneous rock that is typically found in lava flows produced by strato-volcanoes. Since the lava cools rapidly at the surface, these rocks consist of small crystals. As the mineral grains in such rocks are very small in size, magnifying devices need to be used in order to see them.

334 Andesite strato-volcanoes are found in Central America, Washington, Oregon and New Zealand and in other locations above the subduction zones. The rock derives its name from the Andes mountain range situated in South America.

335 It is an interesting thing to know that andesite rocks can form away from subduction environments as well. They can be formed by the partial melting of basalt rocks at ocean ridges and oceanic hot spots. They can also be formed through eruptions at continental plate interiors where deep source magma melts the crust or mixes with continental magmas.

IGNEOUS ROCKS

336 You may be amazed to know that there are rocks on the Moon known as 'lunar maria'. They are so named because scientists have found that the surface of the Moon is underlain by basaltic lava flows and flood basalt rocks.

337 Interestingly, volcanic features on Mars were formed from basaltic lava flows. Olympus mons is a shield volcano and the highest mountain on Mars. It is also considered the largest known volcano in our solar system.

A representation of very high and big volcano Olympus Mons on Mars planet

ROCKS

338 **The Hawaiian Islands were formed by basaltic flows through volcanic cones.** The Big Island has five overlapping volcanoes, of which Kilauea is the most active one. Kilauea is believed to have been the source of as much as one cubic mile of lava through basalt flows, which covers approximately 48 square miles.

339 **Have you heard of the Roman Theatre in Bosra, Syria?** This structure was built using black basalt rocks around the second quarter or second half of the second century A.D. This theatre is considered to be the largest Roman theatre in the Middle East.

340 **Basalt rock is used for a wide variety of purposes.** Crushed basalt is used for making road bases, filter stones in drain fields, railroad ballasts and to cut into dimension stones. Basalt is commonly crushed for use as an aggregate in construction activities.

IGNEOUS ROCKS

341 Have you ever seen coarse-grained rocks with a contrasting mix of black and white mineral grains? This 'salt and pepper' look is of diorite stone. This rock is formed when basaltic magma (that is produced by the partial melting of oceanic plates) is mixed with granite magma or through the melting of granitic rock as the magma rises through continental plates.

342 Diorite is known for its hardness and perhaps this is why early humans often used it to make axes. In the surroundings of the Reims city in France, a Neolithic axe made of diorite was found. It can be seen in the Alexis Damour Collection at the Museum of Toulouse.

343 You may be amazed to know that the Code of Hammurabi is etched upon a seven-feet tall black diorite pillar. This famous pillar was inscribed with Babylonian laws around the year 1750 B.C. It is considered to be one of the oldest deciphered writings of significant length in the world.

ROCKS

344 Although diorite is a hard rock, it has the ability to be polished to a high degree. As such, it is occasionally cut into cabochons or used as a gemstone. A diorite with pink feldspar phenocrysts has been cut into cabochons, and is called 'pink marshmallow stone' in Australia.

345 It is believed that the Earth's oceanic crust is made up of basalt because it has a basaltic composition. However, only a very thin part of this crust comprises basalt; the deeper oceanic crust generally has coarser grained gabbro rocks.

346 At times, gabbro contains trace amounts of some relatively rare metals and hence it can be classified as an ore. Gabbro rocks with high amounts of ilmenite minerals are mined for their titanium content. Sometimes gabbro is also mined to yield nickel, chromium or platinum.

IGNEOUS ROCKS

347 The Yosemite National Park has steep granite cliffs that form the walls of the valley. The geological make up of this area is dominated by granite. The area within the boundaries of this park is made entirely of granite. It has a beautiful natural landscape and provides tourists with the opportunity to explore climbing activities.

348 Have you seen the Mount Rushmore National Memorial? It is a sculpture depicting four famous United States presidents: George Washington, Thomas Jefferson, Theodore Roosevelt and Abraham Lincoln. This sculpture was carved from a granite outcrop on the Black Hills, South Dakota, known as Mount Rushmore. South Dakota historian, Doane Robinson conceptualised this sculpture in order to promote tourism in the region.

349 Scientists believe that one of the first true industries in the world involved tool-making, especially arrowheads, knifes, blades, spear points and scrapers from obsidian rocks, chert or flint. At some locations, the presence of obsidian flakes indicates the existence of ancient 'factories' that manufactured these obsidian tools.

ROCKS

The Scalpel
Blade — Handle

350 **Did you know that rock is sometimes used in surgery?** Obsidian rock produces some of the thinnest and sharpest edges, and as a result, it is used in the production of surgical scalpels.

351 **Fresh pieces of obsidian have very high lustre.** An interesting fact is that early humans used obsidian rocks as mirrors; perhaps they noticed that they could see their reflections in these rocks. To improve the reflective properties of obsidian rocks, people started grinding them flat and polishing them.

352 **Do you know of a park called the Gros Morne National Park in Canada?** This park is home to The Tablelands, made of peridotite rocks from Earth's mantle. It is believed that this structure originated in the Earth's mantle but was thrust upwards because of an ancient plate collision.

IGNEOUS ROCKS

353 You may be amazed to know that in June 1991 there occurred an explosive eruption on Mount Pinatubo, Philippines, which ejected more than five cubic kilometres of material. Most of the material, which blanketed the landscape around the volcano, was pumice lapilli — a type of igneous rocks.

354 At times, ocean-based or near-ocean volcanic activities create a pumice raft — a floating raft of pumice. A 300-mile long and 30 miles wide pumice raft appeared in August 2012, near New Zealand. Similarly, a new island emerged in the South Pacific near Tonga on 12 August, 2006 due to volcanic activities that created a pumice raft.

355 Do you know that pumice stone is considered a good exfoliator for skin? There are many health and beauty products that use pumice as an ingredient. You may have seen brushes with a stone set on one side and a bristle on the other — the stone in this brush is pumice stone, to exfoliate the skin on your feet.

ROCKS

356 Reticulite is a variety of pumice that develops within high lava fountains. With up to 98 per cent porosity, this has the lowest density of any rock. It has a honeycomb-like structure that is created because dissolved gases within the lava form bubbles which expand until they burst. Despite being lightweight, this rock does not float on water.

357 Around the year 126 A.D., Romans constructed the Pantheon using lightweight concrete made with pumice aggregate. In the higher layers of the dome, less dense aggregate stones such as small pots and pieces of pumice have been successively used. This was done to lessen the stresses in the dome.

358 The Crabtree pegmatite of North Carolina is one of the most interesting pegmatites. This granite pegmatite acts as a boundary between two rock units and is up to two meters wide. The Crabtree Emerald Mine was mined by a series of owners for emeralds and many fine clear emeralds were produced, along with emerald-bearing pegmatites that were sold as 'emerald matrix'.

IGNEOUS ROCKS

359 **Lithium can be extracted from the mineral spodumene by fusing in acid.** Each year, around 80,000 metric tonnes of lithium is produced from spodumene, mainly from the Greenbushes pegmatite of Western Australia, as well as some Chinese and Chilean sources. The lithium produced from spodumene is used in many products, such as in ceramics, mobile phones and automotive batteries.

360 **A steep conical hill of loose pyroclastic fragments that is built around a volcanic vent is known as a cinder cone or scoria cone.** The rock fragments are glassy in texture and contain many frozen gas bubbles (called cinders or scoria), which are formed after magma explodes into the air and then cools quickly.

361 **An interesting fact is that scoria stones also exist on Mars.** The Spirit Rover (of NASA's Mars Exploration Rover Mission) found a piece of Martian scoria, measuring around 18 inches in diameter, that most likely had erupted from a Martian volcano. The cinder cones found on the surface of Mars seem to be more than two times wider than those on Earth.

362 **The Sunset Crater is a cinder cone volcano located north of Flagstaff in Arizona, USA.** Created between 1040 and 1100 A.D., it is the youngest among a string of volcanoes related to the San Francisco Peaks.

Metamorphic Rocks

363 **Novaculite is a hard and dense rock.** Native Americans were the first to mine the Arkansas Novaculite Formation for novaculite stone. Perhaps they took notice of its conchoidal fracture and discovered that it could be used to make projectile points, scrappers, weapons and cutting tools.

364 **An interesting fact about Novaculite is that since it is a highly fractured rock unit, it can serve as a suitable aquifer for private water supplies.** Novaculite is mainly found in the Ouachita Mountains in Central Arkansas and Southeastern Oklahoma. In the northern Ouachitas, they are about 60 feet thick and around 900 feet thick in the southern Ouachitas.

Ouachita Mountains

365 **Quartzite is among the most chemically resistant and physically durable rocks found on the Earth's surface.** It is mostly formed during the creation of mountains. As mountain ranges go through erosion and weathering, the less resistant and less durable rocks get destroyed while quartzite survives. Due to this reason, quartzite is often found on the crests of mountain ranges.

METAMORPHIC ROCKS

366 Quartzite is mined for its use in the manufacture of materials like glass, silicon metal, ferrosilicon, silicon carbide, etc. As quartzite has high silica content, it is valued as a raw material. Some unusual deposits of quartzite have up to 98 per cent of silica content.

367 A stone called gneiss is very often labelled 'granite', making it difficult to distinguish between the two. Like granite, gneiss too has an interlocking pattern of grains. As customers do not know the technical names of unusual igneous and metamorphic rocks, gneiss is often marketed as granite in the mineral trading industry.

368 During earlier days, students in elementary schools used slates mounted on wooden frames for writing practice and arithmetic. The pencils used to write on such slates were made of chalk, soapstone or clay. Until the early 1900s, these slates were widely used.

Sedimentary Rocks

369 Polymict breccias or polymictic breccias are a kind of breccia stone that contain many types of rock fragments. For instance, limestone breccias contain multiple types of limestone. Generally, breccia is a very colourful rock. Its colour is determined by the colours of the matrix or cement it contains, along with the colour of the rock fragments.

370 The word breccia means 'loose gravels' and is Italian in origin. Pillow breccias, which are also referred to as volcanic breccias, are formed when lava picks up rock fragments. When the crust of the lava flow is broken up during movement, the breccia so formed is called flow breccia.

SEDIMENTARY ROCKS

371 It is interesting to know that chert is found in many different colours: blue, red, yellow and green. However, if the chert is white, it indicates the presence of impurities like carbonate. If chert contains iron oxide, its colour is red or brown. When chert is of a darker colour, it is referred to as flint.

372 Chert can produce sparks when struck against steel. Due to this property, it was used primarily to make flintlock guns. This firearm had a metal plate which produced a spark when stuck with chert, igniting the charge of gunpowder.

373 According to scientists, some of the oldest mining operations ever discovered were those of chert. It was a precious rock material, as it was not very commonly found. Around the year 8000 B.C., people in present-day England and France dug 300 feet deep shafts to mine chert.

ROCKS

374 **Do you know that coal is also a type of sedimentary rock?** Coal is most often formed in a swamp-like environment because of the accumulation and preservation of plant debris. Coal is one of the three most important fossil fuels, apart from oil and natural gas. The most important use of coal is to generate electricity.

375 **Bituminous coal, also called black coal, is a banded sedimentary rock.** This is a soft variety of coal that contains a tar-like substance called bitumen and has bright and dark bands. While preserved branches or stems form bright bands, the dull bands are formed by mineral materials washed into the swamp by streams, degraded plant materials and charcoal produced during swamp fires.

376 **Coalification is the formation of coal from a variety of plant materials through biochemical and geochemical processes.** The rank of a piece of coal is measured by how much change the plant debris have undergone. This change is also called 'organic metamorphism'. Anthracite has the highest rank among different kinds of coal.

SEDIMENTARY ROCKS

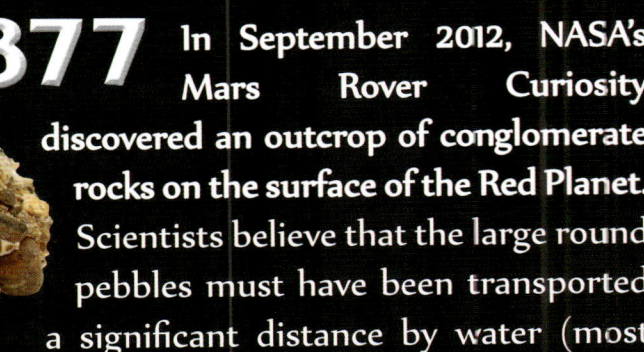

377 In September 2012, NASA's Mars Rover Curiosity discovered an outcrop of conglomerate rocks on the surface of the Red Planet. Scientists believe that the large round pebbles must have been transported a significant distance by water (most likely by a stream) as they are too heavy to be moved by wind.

378 The sedimentary rock dolomite is mainly composed of the mineral dolomite. This rock is also called 'dolostone'. Dolostone also forms the host rock to the double-terminated quartz crystal known as 'Herkimer Diamond'. It has high silica content and is much tougher and harder than typical dolomite.

379 People have been extracting vanport flint for the last 12,000 years. In eastern Ohio, vanport flint outcrop is a layer between one and 12 feet thick, along Flint Ridge. It was used to make a variety of tools and weapons and was traded widely throughout what is now the Eastern United States. People travelled hundreds of miles to collect this rock.

ROCKS

380

An interesting fact is that there are many limestone-forming environments on Earth. Limestone is a sedimentary rock produced by the accumulation of calcium carbonate from sources such as corals, shells, and sea animal and plant debris. They are primarily formed in warm and shallow marine waters. For instance, the whole seafloor of Kerama Island in the East China Sea, southwest of Okinawa, is covered with a wide variety of corals that produce calcium carbonate skeletons. As such, this site has a high concentration of limestone deposit.

381

The world's most significant oil and natural gas deposits have black organic shale as their source rock. Tiny particles of organic matter (from which the shale is formed) give shale its black colour. Over time, mud containing organic debris is buried and warmed within the soil, transforming the debris into oil and natural gas.

382

The word 'silt' refers to loose granular particles that fall within a specific size range. Silt particles are usually thinner and less extensive; they range between 0.00015 and 0.000025 inches in diameter or 0.0039 and 0.0063 millimetres in diameter. You can easily see these stones without the use of a magnifying glass.

NATURAL DISASTERS

Hurricanes

383 A hurricane is a violent storm, often with devastatingly strong winds. Did you know that a 19th century Australian weatherman named Clement L. Wragge started the tradition of naming hurricanes?

384 Hurricanes that occur in the South-Pacific or Indian Ocean are called tropical cyclones. In the northern Pacific Ocean, they are called typhoons. In 1970 in East Pakistan, 200,000 were killed and 100,000 went missing by cyclone-driven tidal waves originating in the Bay of Bengal.

NATURAL DISASTERS

385 Hurricanes form over water bodies. As they start to approach land, they lose their strength. Yet, the devastation they leave behind is unimaginable.

386 Another kind of storm wind system is a tornado. A tornado is a funnel of spiralling winds, with one end touching the Earth and the other in the sky, which may be connected to a storm cloud system. The fastest tornado winds were measured at 286 miles per hour in Texas on 2 April 1958.

387 The longest travelling tornado was spread over a distance of 293 miles on the ground in 1917, where the winds travelled from Missouri to Indiana in USA.

388 A hurricane can hit the coast with wind speeds of over 160 mph. Since it travels over the ocean before it hits land, it can carry more than 2.4 trillion gallons of rain in a single day.

389 Just like they are known by different names in different parts of the world, hurricanes usually form during different seasons as well. Thus, there are different hurricane seasons in the Atlantic and the Pacific. In the Atlantic, hurricane season starts from June 1, while in the Pacific it starts earlier, from May 15. Both seasons usually end by November 30.

NATURAL DISASTERS

390 The hurricane winds build up speeds as they move, finally hitting the land area with such high speeds that they create heavy waves called storm surges, which can easily damage strong buildings.

391 The city of Florida in the US is most commonly hit by hurricanes, with 40% of the hurricanes recorded in the Pacific region occurring in this area alone.

392 A hurricane differs from a simple tropical storm in many ways. Most importantly, hurricanes travel at nearly double the speed of a normal storm.

HURRICANES

393 **The most destructive part of a hurricane is called the 'eye wall'.** This is created by the storm clouds that rotate in a counter-clockwise direction around the centre part of the storm winds called the eye.

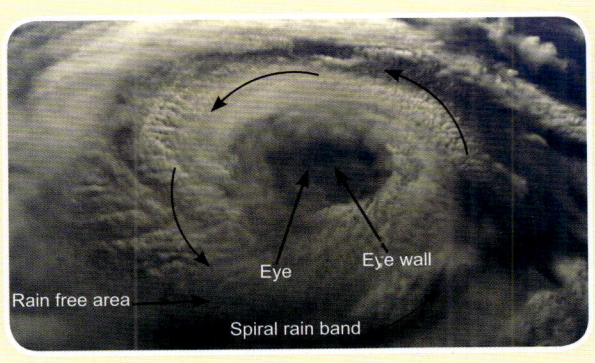

Heavily damaged homes in the Ninth Ward of New Orleans after Hurricane Katrina.

394 **A hurricane that has been very big and destructive is termed as 'retired'.** Retired hurricanes in recent years include Katrina, Andrew, Mitch and the most recent Sandy.

395 **Short names are easier to use than the longer system of naming hurricanes according to latitude and longitude.** It is interesting to note that until 1978, the National Hurricane Center named all storms with women's names. After that, both male and female names have been used.

NATURAL DISASTERS

396 Initially, when two or more storms would take place at about the same time, it would be very confusing to relay information to different weather stations, ships at sea, and coastal bases. Therefore, the National Hurricane Center began giving official names to storms in 1953. Did you know that in the West Indies hurricanes were usually named by the saint's day on which the hurricane appeared?

397 The deadliest hurricane in USA was Hurricane Katrina with damages costing an estimated $108 billion.

Tornadoes

398 A very destructive and powerful form of storm is a tornado. These are spinning winds from a thunderstorm, often with speeds of over 300 mph, that create a rotating funnel shaped cloud.

399 A tornado can damage anything that comes in its path. The spinning force of the winds in a tornado can extend up to one mile wide and for distances as far as 50 miles.

400 Tropical storms and hurricanes originate over the sea, but once on land, the same powerful winds can result in tornadoes. However, the tornadoes do not last for very long, and usually die away within an hour.

401 We can predict tornado activity by keeping a vigil on rotating thunderstorms. These thunderstorms may be accompanied by strong winds, hail, extreme lightening and even flash floods.

NATURAL DISASTERS

402 When a warm front meets a cold front forming a thunderstorm, it takes the form of a tornado. It forms over land, and usually a weather forecaster may not have more than 15-20 minutes warning for its formation!

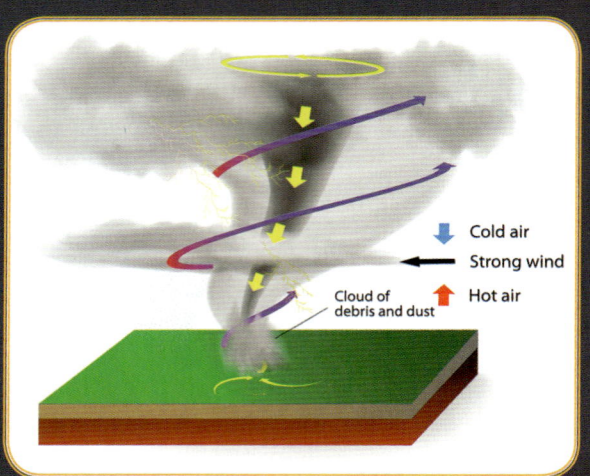

403 Tornadoes are essentially funnels of wind. However, scientists have classified several different shapes of tornadoes. These include conical, cylindrical, and hourglass shaped tornadoes.

404 Did you know that a tornado is nearly transparent until dust and debris gets picked up within the funnel? Tornadoes are rated for their strength using scales called Fujita (F), Enhanced Fujita (EF), and Torro (T) scales.

TORNADOES

405 Do you know which direction a tornado twists? It is fascinating that in the northern hemisphere, tornadoes mostly spin in a counter-clockwise direction, whereas in the southern hemisphere, they spin in a clockwise direction. It is estimated that just 5% of tornadoes spin in the opposite direction to this rule.

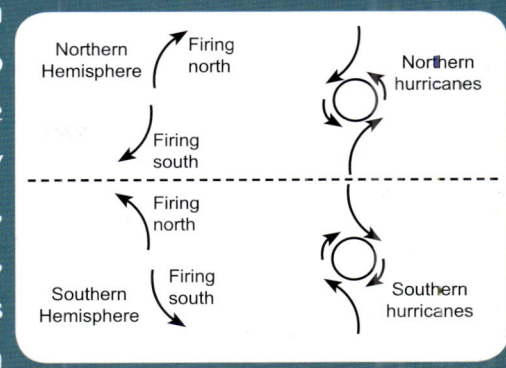

406 Did you know that tornadoes have been spotted in all continents except for Antarctica? The precipitation from a tornado can be in the form of rain, sleet or hailstones. The United States records as many as 1,200 tornadoes in a year, whereas the Netherlands have recorded the densest occurrence of tornadoes, in the smallest area.

- TORNADO
- FLOOD
- EARTHQUAKE
- TSUNAMI
- WILDFIRE
- LANDSLIDE
- VOLCANO
- AVALANCHE
- DROUGHT
- HURRICANE

INFOgraphics
NATURAL DISASTERS

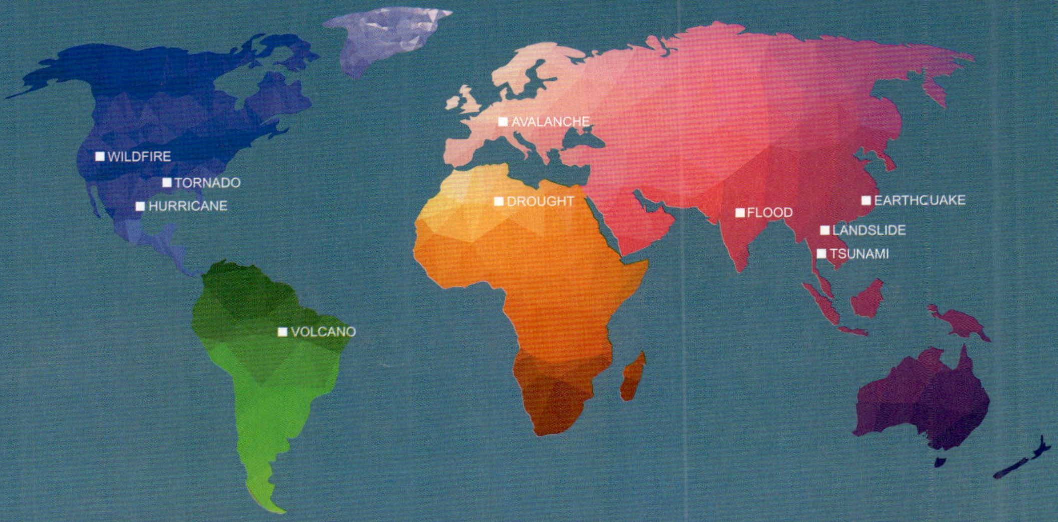

Tsunamis

407 **A tsunami is often caused by tectonic movement underwater.** This can result in very high waves, rising as high as 100 feet. This becomes especially dangerous when the waves hit the shore.

408 **The highest tsunami wave ever recorded reached 278 feet high,** on Ishigaki Island (part of present-day Okinawa) after an earthquake occurred off the coast of Japan in 1771. It caused widespread destruction to buildings and agriculture, and caused the deaths of about 12,000 people.

409 **A tsunami could be caused by an underwater earthquake, landslide, or volcanic eruption.** It could also result from a giant meteor impact with the ocean. The tremors travelling through the water gain speed and intensity, causing huge waves.

TSUNAMIS

410 Did you know that the northern Pacific Ocean has an area of very active tectonic activity, known as the 'Ring of Fire'? It is a horse-shoe shaped area that experiences numerous earthquakes and volcanic activity, often underwater. Because of this, the region also witnesses about 80 per cent of the world's tsunamis.

411 Tsunamis are also called seismic sea waves. Did you know that during a tsunami, the first wave is never the strongest? In fact, each succeeding wave gradually grows stronger and reaches higher.

412 Tsunamis can arise swiftly, and take on speeds as fast as a jet plane! Tsunamis have been recorded to travel at speeds of about 500 miles or 805 kilometres an hour.

413 Tsunamis can travel across the entire ocean without losing much speed and impact, because of minimal energy loss through the water. If you are ever caught by a tsunami wave, don't try to swim, but instead, get hold of a floating object and let the current to carry you.

NATURAL DISASTERS

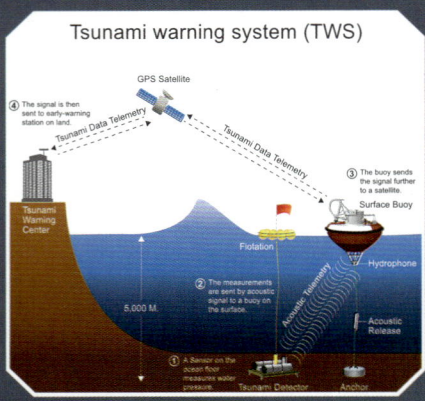

414 While there is a threat of huge waves crashing onto the shore of coastal areas, tsunamis can also cause great destruction through flooding coastal towns. Small islands in the ocean may be completely submerged by a large scale tsunami.

415 In Japanese the word 'tsunami' means 'harbour wave'. The word 'tsu' means 'harbour' and 'nami' means 'wave'. Japan has experienced the longest history of tsunamis, but it was the Greek historian Thucydides who made the connection between tsunamis and oceanic earthquakes.

416 Through years of extensive study, scientists have now managed to identify the preliminary signs of a brewing tsunami. This predictive ability can save many lives in future, as warnings can be sent out to coastal towns. The expected time of a tsunami can be predicted using calculations based on the depth of the water, distances from one place to another and the time when the earthquake struck the region.

TSUNAMIS

417 While Japan is located at one end of the Ring of Fire, the Hawaii islands at the other end also experience regular earthquakes, volcanic activity and tsunamis. It has been observed that they face about one tsunami every year and a severe one every seven years.

418 Hawaii experienced a tsunami in 1960 where Hilo Bay was destroyed. It was hit by 30 feet tall waves at speeds of 500 mph. It was caused by an earthquake that measured 8.5 on the Richter scale, off the coast of Chile.

419 In 2004, there was an even more devastating tsunami that originated in the Indian Ocean. It measured 9.0 on the Richter scale, and its epicentre lay near the west coast of Sumatra.

A 2004 photo of people walking on the debris after the tsunami at Hikkaduwa in Sri Lanka.

NATURAL DISASTERS

420 The 2004 Indian Ocean tsunami hit the coasts of more than 13 countries and caused widespread destruction. The waves were massive, and hit with energy equivalent to 23,000 atomic bombs. Did you know that palm trees can survive the onslaught of tsunami waves?

421 Did you know, it is not necessary that tsunami waves follow one another in rapid succession? The waves come in a series that may be five minutes to an hour apart.

422 Animals can sense an incoming tsunami. Animals fled for higher grounds minutes before tsunami appeared in the Indian Ocean in 2004. Close to 250,000 people died as a result of the tsunami that hit 13 countries on 26 December 2004.

Earthquakes

423 **Earthquakes on land can cause buildings to fall, land to split, and trees to fall.** During an earthquake under the sea, the movement of the Earth's tectonic plates causes such a violent movement that it can displace an enormous amount of water, creating tsunami waves.

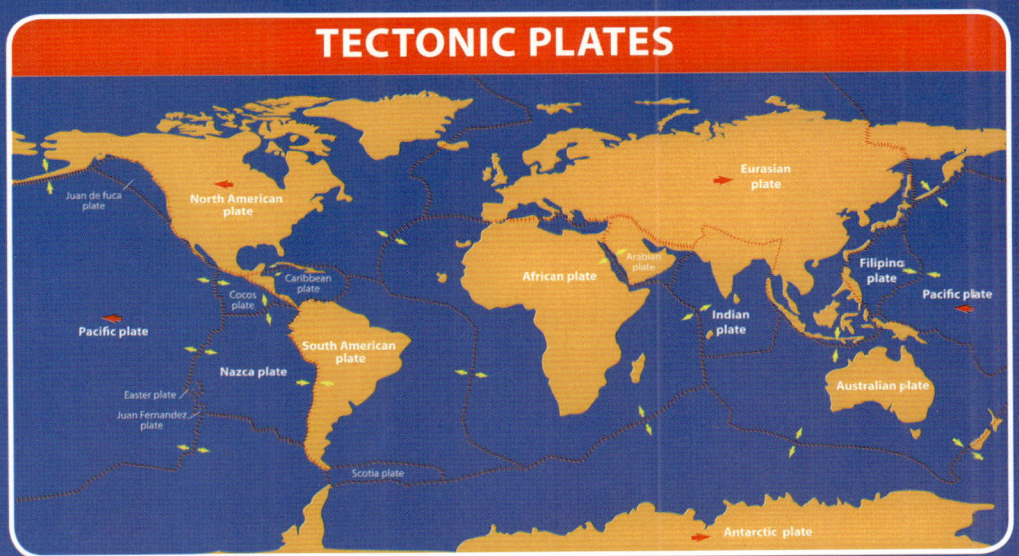

424 **Did you know why John Michell, a writer from the 18th century, is remembered even today?** He was the person who introduced the significant idea that earthquakes are caused due to the movement of the uneven tectonic plates that make up the Earth's crust.

425 **The hypocenter is the point of origin of an earthquake, under the surface of the Earth.** The point directly above it on the surface is called the epicenter. In 2015, Nepal experienced a terrible earthquake, whose hypocenter was just 11 kilometres below the surface. With an intensity of about 7.8 on the Richter scale, it was one of the most damaging earthquakes to strike the region in the past 80 years.

NATURAL DISASTERS

426 The energy generated by the Indian Ocean earthquake in 2004 was so immense that it could have provided power to all the residences and businesses in the United States for three days!

427 Earthquakes can cause major shifts and changes to occur to the Earth's crust. During the 2004 Indian Ocean earthquake, land displacement actually trimmed the Earth's shape near the equator! This was also one of the longest recorded earthquakes, which lasted for about 10 minutes.

428 The San Andreas Fault system is a fault line in the Earth's crust that runs for over 1,280 kilometres, from San Francisco, through southern California, all the way to Mexico. It is a site that frequently gets hit by earthquakes. Scientists have suggested that these frequent tectonic movements could cause such major shifts on land, that San Francisco and Los Angeles will move right next to each other within a period of 15 million years.

EARTHQUAKES

429 The 9.0 Richter scale earthquake in Japan 2011 not only moved the island closer to the United States, but also shifted the Earth's mass toward the center, causing the planet to spin faster! This resulted in shortening the day by 1.6 microseconds.

430 NASA has tested the Real-time Earthquake Analysis for Disaster (READI) Mitigation Network GPS Monitoring System for understanding precise changes occurring in the Earth's crust during massive earthquakes to make accurate and timely tsunami predictions.

431 Earthquakes and tsunamis continue to occur because of the constantly building pressure in Earth's tectonic plates. During a high magnitude earthquake, these tectonic plates can rupture and crack for huge distances, often over 600 miles.

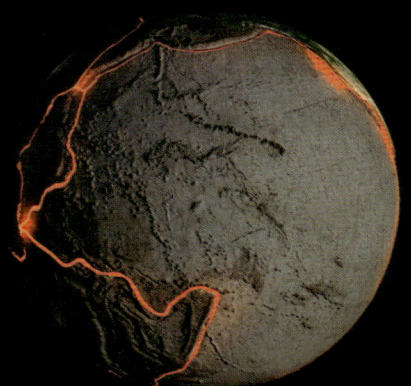 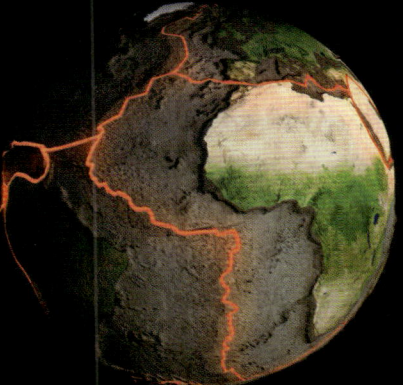

THE EARTH'S FAULT LINES BETWEEN TECTONIC PLATES.

NATURAL DISASTERS

432 During an earthquake, it is not the quake or shaking itself that causes destruction. Most damage is caused by the already-damaged or ill-constructed man-made structures, which buckle and fall during earthquakes.

433 There are actually millions of earthquakes that occur during a year. Most of these are so weak that they cannot be recorded. At an average, it is estimated that we experience around 50 earthquakes every day. Did you know, earthquakes can also be caused by mine tests, volcanic activity, landslides, and nuclear testing?

434 After a strong earthquake, we experience a number of low intensity quakes. These are called aftershocks, and we may feel small tremors for days or even months after a major quake. Aftershocks occur because the displaced fault lines take time to adjust to the changes caused by the main earthquake.

EARTHQUAKES

435 The Ring of Fire zone in the Pacific Ocean is the most vulnerable and earthquake-prone zone, with around 80% of all the planet's earthquakes occurring here. The Ring of Fire is also home to 452 volcanoes, which comprises over 75% of the world's total active and dormant volcanoes.

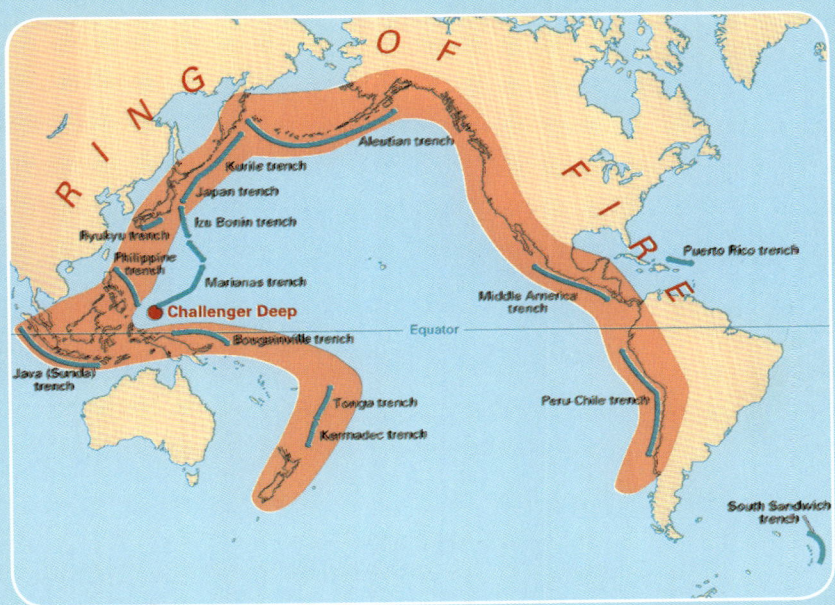

436 With a magnitude of 9.5, the earthquake that struck Chile on May 22, 1960 is the largest recorded earthquake in the world. During the Chilean earthquake, the seismic waves and aftershocks shook the entire Earth for many days.

437 In 1935, American scientist Charles Richter invented the Richter scale. The moment magnitude scale (MMS) was adopted in the 1970s as a method of rating earthquakes based on the energy released.

NATURAL DISASTERS

438 With a magnitude 7.0 earthquake recorded almost every year and a magnitude 8.0 or greater earthquake approximately once every 14 years, Alaska is the one of the most active seismic regions in the USA.

439 Even before we knew the scientific reason for earthquakes, people had come up with numerous stories and myths to explain the phenomenon. One of the Ancient Greek myths blamed the sea God Poseidon for causing earthquakes whenever he struck his trident on the ground! In Hindu mythology, on the other hand, Earth was believed to rest on eight giant elephants, standing on the back of a turtle, which stands on the coils of a snake. Whenever any of these animals moved, it was believed to cause an earthquake!

440 Did you know, the northern hemisphere appears to be more earthquake-prone than the southern hemisphere? Sometimes, earthquakes can cause volcanic eruptions. For instance, in 1980 Mount St. Helens, and in 2002 Mount Etna erupted as a result of earthquakes.

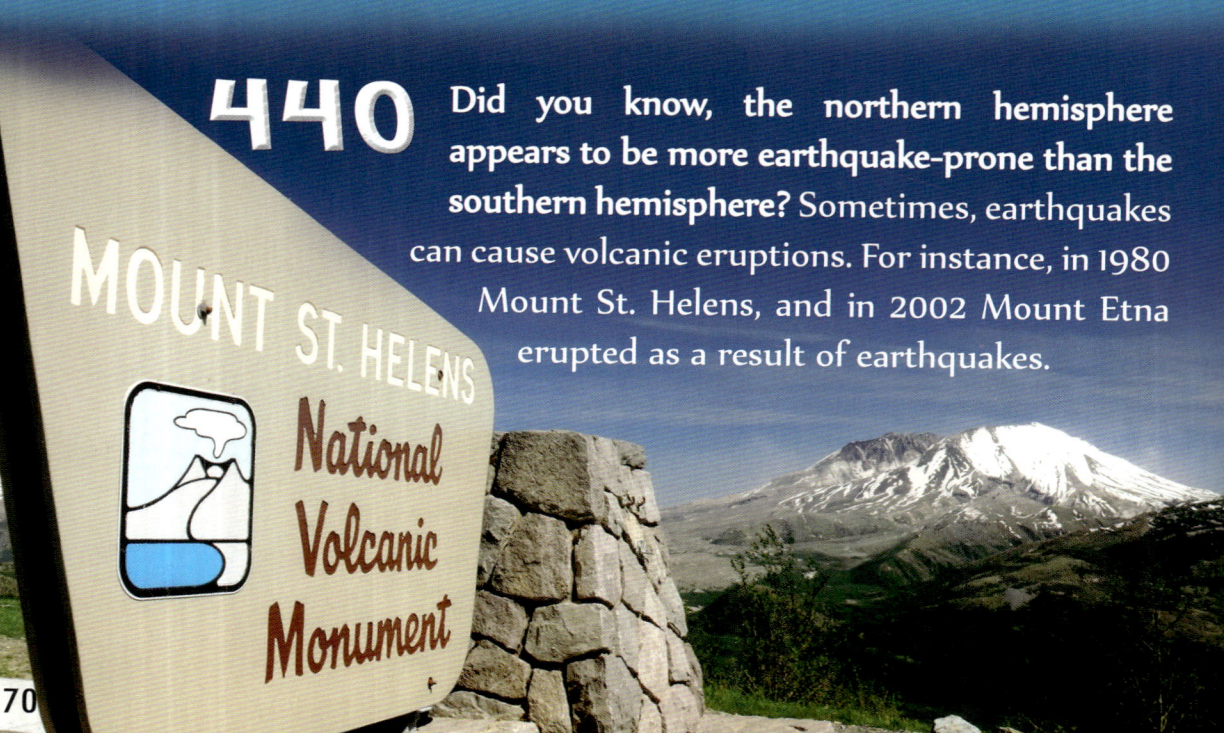

Droughts

441 A drought is a situation where an area faces a severe lack of water. They can occur not only due to a shortfall in rain but also due to lack of moisture in the soil where crops grow.

442 In drought conditions, an additional danger can be of the spread of wildfires. Since the land and vegetation dry up, they can easily catch fire. With lack of water to put out the fire, it can spread, causing further damage and destruction.

Black trees and bushes after a wildfire.

443 Although over 70% of the Earth's surface is covered with water, only about 2.5–3% is freshwater fit for human consumption. About 68% of the world's freshwater is trapped in the ice at the Earth's Poles. As much as 30% of freshwater is present within the soil, as groundwater.

NATURAL DISASTERS

444 Drought is often associated with less or no rainfall. In addition to lack of surface water, this can affect groundwater reserves, making agriculture fail. This in turn, can lead to death for livestock and human populations. A prolonged drought period when crops fail to grow could lead to famine.

445 Whereas the most immediate effect of a drought is seen on vegetation and agriculture, in the long run, it can have terrible effect on human life as well, especially if it results in a famine. For instance, a famine in the Horn of Africa in 1984–85 killed 750,000 people.

446 Deserts are the driest parts of the world, and receive very little rainfall throughout the year. As a result, deserts suffer from a state of constant drought. Even in a desert, however, there are patches of greenery, known as oasis. These arise wherever there is sufficient groundwater to support vegetation.

DROUGHTS

447 **A drought is not a permanent condition.** For instance, the Great Plains of the USA were reduced to a Dust Bowl between 1931 and 1938 due to severe drought. Similar drought conditions were seen in the area again from 1950 to 1954.

Buried machinery in a barn lot in Dallas, South Dakota in 1936. The Dust Bowl extended from Texas into the Northern Plains and Canada.

448 **Human activity often creates drought conditions.** For instance deforestation reduces the soil's water-holding capacity. This dries the ground and leads to a process of desertification. Sometimes, construction of dams for electricity and irrigation to one area can lead to drought downstream, where the flow of water becomes much reduced. Also, air pollution can lead to changes in the climate that affect rainfall, leading to drought in some areas and floods in others.

Avalanches

449 **Avalanche is a general term for a sudden fall of a mass of snow, ice, and rocks down a mountain or hill side.** Did you know that noise does not trigger an avalanche? There are usually four factors that cause avalanches: steep slope, snow, a fissure or weak bond in the snow cover, and a trigger that sets off the avalanche. Though avalanches appear to be sudden, in fact, it is possible to identify warning signs.

450 **When the avalanche is composed only of loose, soft snow, it causes less damage.** An avalanche can be deadly when whole plates or slabs of packed snow slide down mountainsides. These gather speed and mass with collected snow and ice as they slide, thus increasing the scope of destruction. These avalanches are dangerous for any objects or settlements that happen to fall in their path, as well as in the valley below.

AVALANCHES

451 **Avalanches cause an estimated 150 deaths a year.** Often, it is found that the victim triggered the avalanche in some way. Hence, human activity is a major trigger for avalanches. Skiers and snowboarders are particularly at risk of such incidents. Vibration from nearby construction and drilling activities can also act as a trigger.

452 **A steep slope, between 45°–90°, is less likely to witness an avalanche.** A slope of 30°–45° allows snow to build up, which could later slide down as an avalanche. On the other hand, snow on a slope that is flatter than 30° would not slide so easily.

NATURAL DISASTERS

453 Did you know that mountain slopes that are well forested, with a thick tree cover are much safer, and less likely to witness dangerous avalanches? On bare slopes, avalanches are more likely within 24 hours of heavy snowfall, when it measures over 12 inches of snow at a time.

454 If a person is caught in the path of an avalanche, they get buried under a mass of snow. Since the human body is three times more dense than the snow and debris, people tend to sink into the snow. This quickly solidifies and freezes into a hard sheet of ice, trapping them. At that point, it is nearly impossible to even move their limbs.

455 People who are trapped in avalanches have better chances of survival if they are rescued within 15-18 minutes of being trapped. Otherwise, they are likely to perish due to suffocation from being trapped in ice, hypothermia from the cold, or wounds from falling debris.

456 Avalanches can attain speeds of 60–80 mph within five seconds. One of the most horrifying incidents took place on Windy Mountain in Washington state on 1 March 1910. The Spokane Express passenger train was swept away by a wall of ice and snow during a blizzard, right into a 150 feet deep ravine. Despite attempts to save the passengers, 96 people died.

457 **In 1990, an earthquake triggered a deadly avalanche on Lenin peak in the Pamir mountains, at the border of Kyrgyzstan and Tajikistan.** This is counted as one of the most deadly incidents, which completely buried a mountaineering camp, killing 43 out of 140 climbers from around the world.

Trail near the Lenin peak in Pamir Mountains.

Volcanoes

458 **Did you know that a volcano opens up into a pool of molten rock below the Earth's surface?** There are three kinds of volcanoes based on their activity: active, dormant, and extinct. The Kilauea volcano in Hawaii is one of the most active volcanoes on Earth today, as it has been erupting almost continuously since January 1983!

459 **When a volcano erupts, gases and rock fly up through the opening and spill over.** In 1991, Mount Pinatubo in the Philippines erupted, spewing gas and other particles as much as 35 km into the atmosphere. This actually caused global temperatures to go down by about 0.5 degree Celsius the following year.

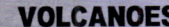

460 Did you know, the Mauna Loa volcano in Hawaii is the largest active volcano in the world? It is 13,677 feet above sea level, but more than 28,000 feet when measured from the ocean floor. When a volcano erupts, a wide area, of at least 20 miles, is considered as part of the danger zone.

461 Volcanic ash consists of rocky particles that are acidic, gritty and smelly. In May 1980, Mount St Helens in the USA erupted, and within nine hours, it had spread as much as 540 million tonnes of ash over an area of roughly 57000 sq kms.

462 When a volcanic eruption is predicted, people living in the area are asked to evacuate well before time. Even after the eruptions stop, the area is not safe to return to immediately. The volcanic ash and particles that linger in the air are dangerous for breathing, and do not settle for days, or even weeks. A volcanic eruption may be accompanied by volcanic lightning as well.

NATURAL DISASTERS

463 A major part of the Earth's surface that we see today has been formed due to volcanic activity. Because of the underlying movement of molten rocks, an erupting volcano can trigger tsunamis, flash floods, earthquakes, mudflows and rock falls.

464 The mid-ocean ridge is a long, uneven chain of volcanic peaks that seem to form a ring around the planet. Scientists believe it formed over the area where several of the Earth's tectonic plates pulled apart. Most of the sea floor, and several undersea mountains were created through volcanic eruptions.

465 The formation of Earth's atmosphere was greatly affected by volcanic activity, as the gases that were emitted by the eruptions added to the mix of gases in the atmosphere. Did you know, there are more than 500 active volcanoes on Earth?

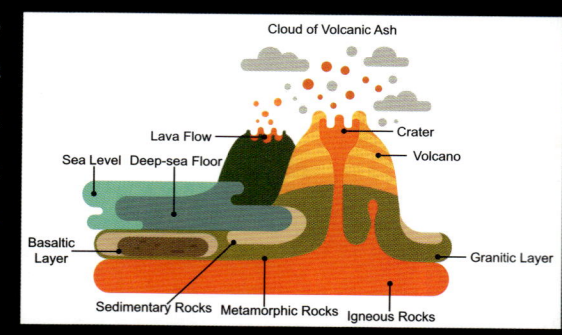

VOLCANOES

466 **More than half of the active volcanoes on Earth are present within the Ring of Fire region around the Pacific Ocean.** Did you know, when a volcano erupts, the sound could be as low as that of a hissing sound and as loud as that of an explosion! However, when the surface of the Earth cracks for lava to spill out, the vibrations and sound can travel hundreds of miles.

467 **The top three countries that see volcanic activity are Indonesia, Japan and the USA.** However, underwater volcanoes are equally active. The West Mata volcano lies in the Lau Basin near Fiji islands, at a depth of about 1,200 metres. Its 2008 eruption is believed to be one of the deepest active eruptions in modern times.

468 **In 1669, a volcanic explosion caused a local war in Italy.** When the citizens of Catania tried to divert the lava flow after an eruption of Mount Etna, their neighbouring villages protested, causing an outright fight to break out!

NATURAL DISASTERS

469 **In May 1902, Mount Pelée in Martinique in the Caribbean islands erupted.** The eruption caused devastation, as about 30,000 people died in the city of Saint Pierre. Even today, though it is no longer active, the volcano does show some signs of seismic activity.

470 **Did you know, the earliest written record of a volcanic eruption was made in Rome in 79 AD by Pliny the Younger, who witnessed the eruption of Vesuvius, just 20 miles away from the volcano!** This was the eruption that destroyed the city of Pompeii, burying it completely under a layer of debris and lava. Pompeii was only rediscovered in 1748.

471 The loudest natural disaster on record was the volcanic explosion in 1833 that destroyed three quarters of the Indonesian island of Krakatoa or Krakatau. At that time, the area was a Dutch colony. The explosion was heard up to 3,000 miles away in Australia, and in Texas, USA! It also resulted in earthquake tremors and tsunamis around the region.

VOLCANOES

472 Have you ever walked barefoot on the ground? The soil feels cool, but just a little distance beneath the surface, the mixture of gases and molten rocks flows at temperatures of 700 degree Celsius to 1,300 degree Celsius!

473 Did you know, not all volcanic eruptions are marked by red and orange hot flowing lava? Sometimes during eruptions, a mixture of hot gases speedily flows down from the sides of a volcano. This looks like a snow avalanche except that it's extremely hot and toxic! This is known as a pyroclastic flow.

474 Can you imagine the coldest place on Earth, Antarctica, is also home to lakes of lava? Antarctica's Mount Erebus is the southern-most active volcano on Earth. It has a pool of molten lava at its mouth, which is one of only five such lava lakes across the world today.

NATURAL DISASTERS

475 We know that volcanoes are found on land and on the ocean floor, but did you know, they can exist even under icecaps, such as those found in Iceland? One of the largest eruptions of the 20th century was seen in Alaska, when Novarupta erupted in 1912. It was ranked at six on the Volcanic Explosivity Index, where the maximum intensity can be eight!

476 Have you ever wondered about the composition of the gaseous emissions from volcanic vents? Water vapour is the most abundant volcanic gas, followed by carbon dioxide, sulphur dioxide and other volcanic gases like hydrogen sulphide, hydrogen chloride, and hydrogen fluoride.

477 Volcanoes can be very unpredictable and sometimes give no warning before eruption, like the Arenal Volcano in Costa Rica, which erupted suddenly in February 2010. On the other hand, sometimes, gas and ash may be spewed beforehand, indicating an upcoming eruption. However, even that is not a sure indication, as seen in Mount Cleveland in Alaska, which released a plume of thick ash, indicating an eruption, but did not actually erupt!

VOLCANOES

478 Can you think of any benefits we could reap from volcanoes? The island nation of Iceland has 35 active volcanoes, and has harnessed plentiful geothermal power from the heat that emanates from the volcanoes.

479 You will be amazed to know that the Earth is not the only planet in the Solar System to have volcanoes. The largest volcanoes in the solar system are the giant shield volcanoes on Mars. They are comparable to a pile of 100 Hawaiian volcanoes on Earth!

480 Geologists have studied the crust of the Earth and estimated that a violent prehistoric eruption may have caused a section of the Earth's crust to collapse. This formed a crater that then filled with water and gas that bubbled up from the bottom. This natural wonder is today called the Laacher See (or Lake Laach) in Germany.

NATURAL DISASTERS

481 Did you know, the female Maleo bird from the Indonesian island of Sulawesi buries its egg in the heated soils around a volcano? The natural heat of the volcano acts as the ideal nest for incubation.

482 The Barren Island in Andaman and Nicobar Islands is the only confirmed active volcano in South Asia. This volcano is labelled as a stratovolcano, and experiences both lava and pyroclastic emissions.

483 Can you visualise volcanic activity in the pristine white glaciers of Iceland? The hard to pronounce Eyjafjallajökull volcano is an active sub-glacial volcano in Iceland. In 2010, this volcano erupted, and the ash caused such a dense cloud to form that it seriously disrupted air traffic across Europe.

Floods

484 Just as lack of water is a problem, an excess of water either through heavy rainfall, tsunamis, or sea floods is equally destructive. For example, in 1228 in the Netherlands, 100,000 people were drowned by a sea flood in Friesland. Similarly, the flood along Yangtze River in China in 1931 left 3.7 million people dead from disease, starvation, or drowning.

485 In 1953, the Queen of England was in New Zealand. At that time, the country experienced one of their greatest natural disasters, when a flood caused a mudslide that demolished the Tangiwai Bridge, killing 151 passengers on board a train.

486 Did you know that the earliest civilizations grew along river valleys that experienced annual flooding? The floods spread fertile silt across the land, encouraging agriculture. For instance, the Mesopotamian civilization flourished along the Tigris-Euphrates, Egyptian civilization along the Nile, and the early Indian civilizations along the Indus and Ganges.

487 **Did you know, the Yellow River (Huang He) in China is also called China's sorrow?** This is because the river has witnessed the four deadliest floods in world history, killing people, animals and destroying settlements.

488 **Floods have caused great destruction, but they are also part of most civilizations' mythologies.** For instance, a great flood is mentioned in the Legend of Gilgamesh of Ancient Mesopotamia, in the Genesis story of Noah's Ark, and in the Matsya Purana legends of India.

Extreme Temperatures

489 All living beings require a certain optimal temperature range to live. However, global fluctuations can cause unusually cold or hot weather situations. Did you know that there was a snowflake that was 15 inches wide and 8 inches thick fell in Fort Keogh, Montana in 1987? This was the largest snowflake recorded, and is listed in the Guinness World Records.

490 Did you know, the persistent fear of snow, especially of being trapped by snow, is known as chionophobia? It is often seen in people who have faced traumatic experiences such as injuries in snow, often in childhood.

491 In 1888, north-eastern America experienced a terrible blizzard, also known as the Great Blizzard or Great White Hurricane. It affected most of the east coast, from Canada in the north, down to Virginia in the south. It severely affected railways and telegraph services, wrecked ships, caused flooding, and damaged property. Further, the cold killed over 400 people.

NATURAL DISASTERS

492 **Do you know the coldest spots on Earth?** The lowest temperature in any inhabited area was recorded at minus -68 degree Celsius at Oymyakon, Siberia on 6 February 1933 and at Verkhoyansk in Siberia, on 3 January 1885.

493 Just as low temperatures are dangerous, similarly, very high temperatures are also undesirable. The highest recorded temperature on Earth was 58 degree Celsius in El Azizia, Libya, in September 1922.

494 **The Ice Age is a phenomenon that began about 2.6 million years ago, where the global temperature dropped drastically, causing the ice cover to spread from the Poles towards the equator.** Most creatures had to quickly adapt to the new weather conditions to survive. Thus, animals such as woolly mammoth and sabre-tooth tigers emerged. They died out when the temperatures became warmer again. Did you know that we are currently believed to be living in an inter-glacial period?

Wild Fire

495 Wildfires are uncontrolled blazes that spread very fast, especially when fuelled by dry underbrush. It is estimated that wildfires can spread at a speed of up to 23 kilometres an hour. The fire can incinerate everything in its path, be it vegetation, buildings, or even humans and animals. Did you know, 90% of all wildfires are started by human activity?

496 Did you know, the spark to start a wildfire can come from a variety of sources—burning campfires, cigarettes, lightning, hot winds, or even sun rays? In 1996, a wildfire caused by high winds and hot temperatures in the foothills around Boise, Idaho, burned for seven days.

497 In areas that are prone to wildfires, fire fighters have to be prepared beforehand to prevent massive destruction. Some methods of firefighting are dousing with water and using fire extinguishers. To slow or stop spreading fires, two methods that are used are clearing vegetation in the path of the fire, or creating firebreaks.

NATURAL DISASTERS

498 Did you know, wildfires also play a positive role in nature? By burning the vegetation and decaying matter, **they return nutrients to the soil.** By removing diseased plants and harmful insects, they clear the forest ecosystem. Further, they clear the underbrush, allowing fresh, new seedlings to grow.

499 Wildfires don't always burn only the underbrush. When the wind spreads the fire swiftly among the tops of trees, it is known as a 'crown fire'. Running crown fires can be very deadly, as they travel swiftly, changing directions with the wind.

500 In April 1906, San Francisco was hit by an earthquake of about 7.8 magnitude. It destroyed underground waterpipes and broke several gas pipes, and fires broke out across the city. The fires raged for four days, destroying large areas of the city completely. Apart from the naturally spreading fires, some people actually set fire to their houses which had been damaged by the earthquake. This was because they wanted to claim insurance, and at that time, insurance did not cover earthquakes!